The Art of Casting a Fly

A Treatise

Paul Argentini

Vera C. Argentini, Artist

HEARTH & HOME PRESS

an imprint of Sunbury Press, Inc.
Mechanicsburg, PA USA

an imprint of Sunbury Press, Inc.
Mechanicsburg, PA USA

For information about special discounts for bulk purchases, please contact Sunbury Press Orders Dept. at (855) 338-8359 or orders@sunburypress.com.

To request one of our authors for speaking engagements or book signings, please contact Sunbury Press Publicity Dept. at publicity@sunburypress.com.

FIRST HEARTH AND HOME EDITION: June 2020

Set in Adobe Garamond | Interior design by Crystal Devine | Cover by Lawrence Knorr | Edited by Lawrence Knorr.

Publisher's Cataloging-in-Publication Data
Names: Argentini, Paul, author. Argentini, Vera C., artist.
Title: The art of casting a fly : a treatise | Paul Argentini Vera C. Argentini, artist.
Description: Trade paperback edition. | Mechanicsburg, PA : Hearth and Home, 2020.
Summary: Experienced author and fly fisherman Paul Argentini explains the techniques for successfully casting a fly, mixed with his wisdom of many years in streams seeking trout.
Identifiers: ISBN 978-1-620068-55-7 (softcover).
Subjects: SPORTS & RECREATION / Fishing | SPORTS & RECREATION / Outdoor Skills.

Product of the United States of America
0 1 1 2 3 5 8 13 21 34 55

Continue the Enlightenment!

Also by this best-selling author

Fiction

The Fourth Nail – An Historical Novel

Jim – A War-torn Love Story

Non-Fiction

Elements of Style for Screenwriters
The Essential Manual for Writers of Screenplays
Random House Bestseller

MUSICALS! Directing School and Community Theatre
Robert Boland and Paul Argentini

Full-Length Plays

The Essence of Being

King's Mate

Massachusetts Artists Foundation
Playwriting Fellowship

One Act Plays

No Gas For Nick

Pearl Seed

My Pen Name's Mark Twain
(written and performed in sixth grade)

Theatre Odyssey 2011 Ten-minute Play Festival
The Ordinance – First Prize Winner
Sarasota, Florida

The Essence of Magnitude

VERA ARGENTINI's work is in private and corporate collections in the U.S. and abroad. A prize-winning watercolorist, she illustrated *The Berkshire Flower Watch* by C.E. Clark, and the weekly *Flower Watch* column, by C.E. Clark in the *Berkshire Record*.

To Mona Claire Argentini,
the personification of what all good
and superior human beings should be.

It's more fun to master short lines and a couple flies
than have scads of 'em and long, botched up casts.

—The author

Theme:

"A Song Of Peace"
Hymn written by Lloyd Stone (1912-1993)
using the Finlandia Hymn melody composed
by Jean Sibelius (1865-1957)
(If, while fly-fishing, one listens closely
one will hear this very clearly.)

Learn to fly-fish,
then you will have a best friend
for the rest of your life,
which also will teach you
things about yourself
because it always works
the truth.

—Paul Argentini

Contents

Illustrations

Brother Dino (left) and author, opening day of fishing season, 1957,
Great Barrington, Massachusetts.

Introduction

My dear reader, no one can teach you how to cast a fly except yourself. That's a fact. I'll show you how, but you must do it hands-on. I have read dozens upon dozens of explanations of how to cast a fly. Those that explain and micro-manage every inch of the cast just plain take the fun out of all of it.

The most fun answer I have for you if you wish to learn how to cast a fly is to find a friend who knows how to fly-cast and spend a little time together doing it. The next best answer I have for you is to read this treatise. The absolute best answer is to read this treatise and then find a friend who knows how to fly-cast.

Fly-casting is not challenging to learn. If you start correctly from the beginning, and progress slowly, it's easy. What is difficult is taking the time to understand how to do it, and everyone—especially if you're a fisherman—has the patience to do that.

Because fly casting is a physical thing, we must deal with physics. Certain elementary principles of physics must be understood to be most successful in casting a fly. They will be explained in as plain a manner as possible, which hopefully everyone can understand. Once these principles are clear to you, the next step is for you to make personal adjustments to them.

The first adjustment is to allow the use of "his" and "her" interchangeably. Fly-fishing is all about making adjustments in every way all the time every moment you are fishing, whether you're a novice or expert. As in life, when you believe you know everything there is to know about anything, you will find another lesson to learn.

You will not ever face the same conditions twice. The more experience you acquire, the more you will understand exactly what adjustments are to be made and how to make them. To mention a few things that will get your attention: how you stand; the weather; the wind; the water; the fish; the geography; and we've yet to mention the equipment or your disposition—and because you are fly-fishing it will improve.

You are unique. Your reaction time, your strength, your height, weight, nimbleness, dexterity, and other capacities, are all peculiar and particular to you. An instructor or fly-fishing school can only take you so far, but the critical adjustments are entirely up to you. A little faith in your capacity, and you will become your own master in the art of casting a fly. I guarantee you will be a master. The reason I can do this is that you need only to satisfy yourself in every and all respects. Because you are unique, I address and dedicate this book to you. As a student, I accept you totally as you are. I'm sure—and hope—this is not the only fly-fishing book you have read. I'm sure every instructor truly believes he or she has the perfect instructions. I sense the others are writing to the ideal student. Fly-casting can't only be done one way. The ramifications of handling a fly-line are enormous. My philosophy is to give you the basics, which you will adapt to your ability and understanding. I say you must do what is comfortable for you.

Only then can you enjoy what is meant to be enjoyed. I'm not going to try to convince you to use a confining wrist strap when you may find it as useful as eating soup with a fork. Should things go astray for you, my answer is to go back to the basics to teach yourself. I will show you how to snap a fly off a line, so if you find yourself feeding flies to the air, you will understand how to correct it. I was told never to bend my wrist when I was playing tennis, yet, when I taught myself how to time a snapped wrist when I hit a tennis ball, I was sending zingers over the net. Not right, not wrong, just me. The same as fly-fishing should be about you. Bend your wrist, don't bend your wrist is answered first by how it works best for you. Do what's comfortable. If you need to go to an instructor for a particular aspect, pay attention but make the art your own.

Once you understand what's going on, you will know what to do, and you will learn to make adjustments so that everything happens just as you wish it. Be patient with yourself. It's easier than you think.

Your mindset when you are fly-casting is somewhat like that of a big-league batter stepping up to the plate. He must be present—alert is more like it—every single fraction of a second, he's there. Every single ball thrown to him may be called a "ball," or a "strike," or even be hit by him for a home run, or the pitched ball could hit him! Not paying attention can be costly. Even though you may not have as much at stake as a ballplayer, how much fun you have depends on how alert you are while you're fly-fishing. If you're using garden hackle (worms) and a bobber, you can fish and snooze in the boat. If you are fly-fishing, the relaxation comes in the doing: the anticipation, the getting there, the preparation, reading the water, selecting a fly, and presenting it to the elusive fish.

For thirty-five years, I have taught only how to cast a fly. Everyone who came to me learned at no charge. It usually took a short time, depending on how much they brought to the table. Many, after trying and trying with paid lessons and all, still couldn't manage to cast a fly. In many cases, I was their last resort. The look on their faces after working with me and making several false casts in a row was a rewarding sight to see. I love to fly-fish. I know this world would be a better place if everyone in the world fly-fished. I'm doing my bit by writing this treatise. Take from it what works for you and discard the rest. There's a boatload of books to read.

The crux of fly-casting technique for me is summed up in one sentence:

WAIT UNTIL THE LINE IS STRAIGHT.

If you come to understand that, and can do it, you don't need this book.

In teaching, I simply took the mystery out of what had to happen to get things going right. I could do it because I knew exactly what was going on, and I could explain it in student terms to the student. In turn, when the student understood the principles, that student made his adjustments and made the art his or her own. I like that. You'll like it, too.

The key to unlocking the wonderful world of fly-fishing is the cast.

Learning to cast a fly starts with understanding the physics involved. From there, it's a very simple physical thing to do. It is so important I've devoted instructions in this book only and entirely to the art of casting a fly.

Also presented in this treatise are some of the incredibly beautiful works of art the fly fisherman uses in his sport, the artificial flies and lures, which in this book we'll say mean the same thing. To broaden the understanding of the art of fly-fishing, also presented are entomological, terrestrial, and man-made examples of what may be on the fish's menu. When the fly-fisherman sees the fish are dining on any of these naturally available foods, then the art of fly-fishing is heightened even more by his choice of the right-sized artificial fly that is tied so perfectly it resembles the actual thing and fools the wary fish. One of the nicest phone calls to get from a friend: "Get your fishing gear! There are hatches of Blue-winged Olives on the river!" The action is even more ephemeral than life.

An aside about the artwork in this volume concerns Vera's request for me to bring her a live brook trout so she could get the colors exactly right. In front of

PLATE A. BLUEGILL SUNFISH

our home was a little stream that was a refuge for trout that came up from a small pond. I caught a brookie and put it in a bucket for her. It reminded me of another time when my older brother, Dino, who was about seven years old at the time, showed me how he lay down beside a brook, let his bare arm "drift" in the water, and would catch trout with his bare hand. He was a child of Nature. As I grew to understand this, I knew every human on Earth was a steward of our world. It seems especially every day we should all do our part.

There will always be someone who believes their way of teaching fly-casting is better. It very well may be. If you don't understand what I'm trying to say, don't deprive yourself of this marvelous sport and by all means, do try other methods or schools until you get it.

Only because they are around, I must mention that there are gadgets available to teach fly casting. New paraphernalia comes on the market all the time. One thing is certain about them: they work for their inventors.

I feel the myriad of other things to learn about fly-fishing—knot-tying, reading the water; how to fish a rill, a brook, a river; the art of caddis fishing; how to tend to flies; and on and on; had better be left to the experts who have their own books to write. Check them out, too.

When my students wanted to know the reason things went as they did in fly-casting, I offered them a reasonably good explanation, which I have incorporated in this treatise.

Another point, once you can help someone else learn to fly-cast, you may realize there were some points I didn't cover. Try as I might, I couldn't get to them all because many of these situations will be unique to you and the best way you know how to derive pleasure from this sport. You might say, "Oh! A hip bucket is a better way to keep line I've stripped in because I can shoot the line easier when I must do that." Now you are custom tailoring this sport to suit you exactly, which is precisely what you should do. My goal is to open the main door to this sport. For all the others, you must check things out. As the Scotsman says, "You pays your money and takes your choice."

There are many facets to the art of fly-fishing besides casting the line. For one, because it is so vital, I include in this treatise an introduction to the art of choosing what to tie on the end of a fly-line. I'll repeat, flies and lures catch more fishermen than fish. A fly may appear as a beautiful work of art, well made, and attractive to the fisherman. It may represent last week's liver and onions to the fish, however. A footnote to choosing a fly is the fact that not only is a fish smart enough to untie a knot, but a fish will not go after food that will not give it back more in energy than it takes to catch it. Knowing that makes it clear the reason accuracy in fly-fishing is so important.

A heads-up, a clue on what fly to use would be where you are fishing—a brook, a stream, a river, a lake—what time of day you are fishing—morning, noontime, or night—and what season. Of major import is if you can accurately determine what fish food is readily available. "Matching the hatch" is part of this scenario.

To touch on flies quickly, they are classed as either imitative or attractors. Imitatives resemble the food fish find naturally. Attractors trigger instinctive strikes because that's what fish do just as a bull will charge a red cloth waved before it. Flies include surface dry flies; those known as emergers, which are partially submerged; or fished underwater, such as wet flies, nymphs, streamers. Included in this book are entomological drawings (insects found naturally in the water), larvae, nymphs, and pupae, baitfish, crayfish, leeches, worms. Wet flies, others known as streamers, are generally thought to imitate minnows, leeches or scuds, and terrestrial (land-based species that fall into the water) representations of what may be on a fish's menu.

Study them.

Stand quietly by the water for a few minutes. Ask yourself what you see. Kick some rocks in the water aside. Check out if there are shell casings, hatchings of any kind. If you can recognize what food the fishes are eating your skill in selecting a fly that most closely resembles, it is vastly improved. What colors will induce a strike comes from experience and by-guess and by-gosh. Included are drawings of actual classic flies that have been handed down through generations. Some were ratty-looking and the worse for wear, faded, with only bits of the floss left on the hooks. Some are still being tied and used. The fish don't appreciate their antiquity, but true fly-fishermen do. Flies and lures in themselves are works of art and are included just for that. With apologies, we'll call our presentations merely a bit of sampling. Representations of classic flies may be harder to find, so we've included them. I agree that they should be displayed in museums, but the fact is they work better at the end of a fly-line.

On the water, combine choosing the right fly or lure to use with the art of presentation, and you are in for a great deal of fun, which is what fly-fishing is meant to be. I'll try to keep it that way for you.

With fly-fishing, as it is with sailing, or tennis, or life when you feel you know it all, you will find there is one more lesson to learn.

—Paul

1

Fly Fishing

You can only enjoy the magnificent world of fly-fishing if you can cast a fly.

Casting is the key to acquiring the life-long enjoyment of fly fishing. It's the reason I focus on casting the fly.

You are going to read how to fly-cast.

If you want to learn how to fly-cast or learn how to do it better, you may wish to read this treatise.

Fly-casting is an art and a science.

This means some aspects are cast in brass. That's what they are. Amen. And there are other aspects of this sport in which you will need to develop your special knack to master them. Let's say there's more fun in art than there is in science. And there's more fun in getting there rather than in the arriving.

It all begins in the classroom. You must understand what you are trying to do and how to go about doing it. Once you get this, the art comes with it—hand in glove.

Learning to fly-cast starts with appreciating what is going on and the reasons it works the way it does. I ask for your patience as we proceed step by step, especially if you know the material, and it gets repetitious. I'm not writing this to bore you, but you must slug your way through the brambles to get to the berries. I must write this for the hopeful fly-fisherman who is putting the information on a blank page, not for the expert tweaking his skill.

Here we go.

Let's come to terms with terms.

Angle or angling means to fish with a hook. It also means to use artful means to gain an objective. Now there's a perfect definition of a fisherman who uses everything within his means to catch a fish. That includes live and artificial lures of all sorts; fly-fishing, invisible lines, and artifices of every means and manner. If I again may editorialize, flies and lures have caught more fishermen than fish; and based on results of fishermen fishing and fish caught, the fish appear to be much, much smarter. Although, whatever the outcome, the fishermen seem to be much happier.

The greatest type of fishing that produces the most fun is whatever kind of fishing the fisherman prefers. But, rating all the fishermen by what measure of joy each type of fishing induces, and the time, energy, and expense to do it unquestionably the gold reel goes to fly-fishing. Learn to fly-fish, and you will be its willing slave for life.

We speak about **FLY** fishing just as we would talk about a bird flying.

The line used in fly fishing is called a **fly line** because when it is cast or thrown, it flies.

It is called a **fly rod** because it is a vital part of the art of flying a line to fly-fish.

The lure in fly fishing is called **a fly** simply because it is used in fly fishing, it flies, and some say because it is as light as a fly.

It is called fly fishing because only by flying a line through the air can one cast a near weightless fishing lure—a fly—some distance.

Fly fishing is used to cast a fly because it enables the fisherman to present a fly in its most natural form and in its most natural way. An adequately cast fly fools a fish into thinking the lure is edible, which entices the fish into trying to eat it and gets caught instead. Okay, I understand, at times a sporting fish will strike at a lure in anger or just for the fun of it because that's what game fish do.

When we speak of **FLY** fishing, we are primarily talking about the fly line.

It is called a fly line because the line flies like a bird.

It is called fly fishing because when we use a fly rod and a line to cast a fly, the line is cast or thrown in the air. As a bird flies, so does the line.

Before you can put a fly in the air by casting it, you need a substantial amount of related information. Bear with me.

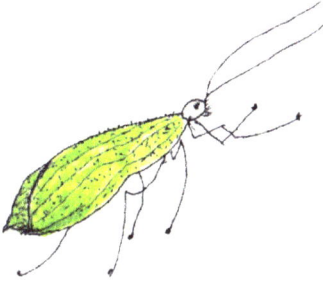

2. CADDIS FLY

3. CADDIS – LARVAE

4. CADDIS – LARVAE CASES

5. CRANEFLY –
LARVA

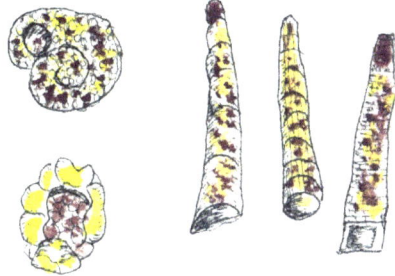

6. CRANEFLY – PUPA

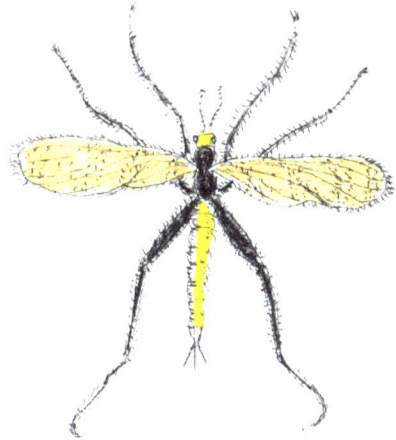

7. CRANEFLY – ADULT

2

Equipment

The fly-fishing rod has dominant supreme qualities that go far beyond other rods. It must be supple and be durable enough to take many years of bending and springing back and forth and back and forth to cast and carry a fly line.

Among the earliest materials were greenheart, a tropical wood, and bamboo. It was discovered that when bamboo was manufactured: split, formed into sections, heated, and rejoined into six- or eight-sided graduated parts of a rod, it eminently satisfied the needs of a light, supple, long-lasting fly-casting rod. The art of hand-crafting a bamboo rod has progressed to where a hand-made, signed copy may fetch its weight in gold. Since then, other materials have been used from glass, to fiberglass, to modern composites, to high-tech graphite rods. Prices vary. Today in some large discount stores, a fly rod may run as little as twenty dollars. A commercial composite may run $250.

No matter what price or size of rod you use, the art and technique in casting a line for short or long distances remains the same.

Fly-rod types are many. Most fly-fishing catalogs will list dozens upon dozens. There are one-piece rods, and they progress to two-piece rods that vary in lengths up to around nine feet, with the blanks—the plain rod without reel holder, handle, ferrules, guides—weighing two ounces and up. There are four- and eight-piece suitcase (so-called because they'll fit in one) rods, and combinations that are convertible—or double in brass—for use both as a fly-casting rod or as a spinning rod.

A popular bamboo fly rod is eight-and-a-half feet long in three pieces. The rod may come with two "tippets," which are the topmost or thinnest sections of a graduated three-piece fly rod. One tippet will be less supple than the other for playing larger fish and a thinner tippet for smaller fish, such as brook trout, sunfish, panfish, or to meet the circumstances of fishing, like wind conditions. There is another reason for having two tippets, which is simply because—for whatever reason—it is easier to change the tippet than it is to switch to a lighter or heavier line. I believe today they don't as much change the rod's tippet or the line as the change to a completely different rod. Besides, it's good to have an extra one because rod tippets have a strange way of getting slammed and broken in car doors. Fly-rods of modern materials generally are made in two-pieces.

Fly rods are stored in a sectioned carrying bag, cardboard or metal or plastic tubes, or round or flat wooden carriers to protect them. Some are made with room for an attached reel. Old-timers stored bamboo rods by putting them together and suspending them from the topmost guide to keep them straight.

A fly rod is made up of:

- At the bottom of the rod is the reel seat with a mechanical system—either sliding or threaded ring—to hold the reel, which stores the fly line and backing.

- A handle, usually of cork or foam, made in different shapes for individual preferences.

- A "keeper" or hook keeper just above the handle on the rod as a convenient place to store the fly still tied to the line.

- Just below the first joining ferrule is a heavy-duty stripper guide, which takes the brunt of stripping line in or shooting line out.

- Ferrules are matching male and female parts usually made of metal or plastic that are used to join sections of a rod.

- The guides are evenly spaced and attached to the rod to keep line orderly going in and out and to prevent the line from tangling (more guides is not necessarily better because they may affect the rod's action).

- Single- or double-foot snake guides—so-called because of their shape—or circular guides, which are attached to the rod with thread or plastic windings with single-foot guides preferred because the single wrappings affect the rod's action the least, which you couldn't prove by me;

- Underwrappings are protection used as a base to hold wrapped guides especially single-foot, which allow for greater flexibility in the rod; and

- The tip-top guide is usually heavy-duty because it also takes the brunt of stripping in the line or shooting it out.

When a fly rod is manufactured, its weight and suppleness are determined and are assigned the weight of the fly line to be used with it. At one time, the weight of lines was given alphabetical letters. Today the system uses single numbers adopted by the American Fishing Tackle Manufacturers Association (AFTMA) for the sake of uniformity.

Simply as a matter of incidental information, the specific numbers assigned to a line describe the weight of the first thirty feet of the line less the level tip of the line. Thus, today, an AFTMA No. 6 line weighs 160 grains for a double taper (DT) HDH (old style) line and a Weight Forward line at HDG. A No. 7 weighs 195 grains with a DT (double taper) labeled HCH and a WF (weight forward) at HCF. This all sounds like very technical bafflegab, but what does this mean to the novice fly-fisherman? It means nothing is cast in bronze just yet. In time you may need to know.

There is no reason to use a weight line other than the one marked on a rod by the manufacturer. The recommendations are for a line matched to a rod. Are there circumstances where a permanent line change is called for? Yes, indeed, but it is rare. It's easier to use a lighter or heavier tippet if you have one that came with the rod. Also, if you are competent in casting a line, you simply adjust.

Adjusting above everything else is the foundation for fly fishing. Why have a line matched to a rod in the first place? Because the spring action of the rod works best moving and carrying that certain weight of line back and forth and back and forth. A bad example is a bow using bakery string is not going to send a heavy arrow far. This is comparable to a screen door using a strong spring to make it shut with a Bam! If it's not the right line for the rod for you, then you're not using the correct rod, so change both for a matched unit. It usually will work better together and for you.

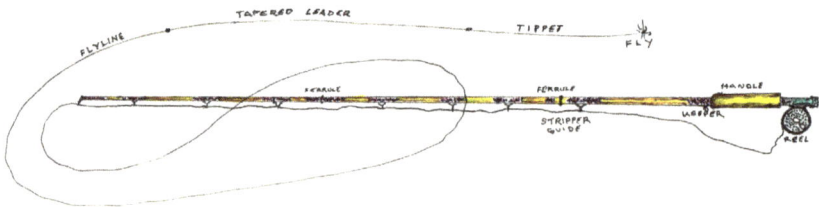

1. TWO-PIECE FLY CASTING ROD

12

The importance of the fly line cannot be emphasized enough. For the beginner, the primary information about a line is the core, the coating, the taper design, and the line weight. The core determines the tensile strength and stretchability of the line. The coating determines the performance of the line, which means castability, shoot-ability, and durability. For the beginner, this is simply incidental information.

Lines are floating or sinking.

At one time after use, fly lines were stretched between posts, wiped down and air dried, and then waxed to ensure that they floated. This was a lot of work. Such stuff is outdated, ancient history. Today the floating lines are water-resistant, which allows them to float higher. The sinking lines are denser for a certain distance at the end, which will enable them to drop below the surface very quickly.

The general rule is floating lines are used for dry flies that are fished on top of the surface. Sinking lines are used for wet flies that are fished underwater.

The most popular fly line in use is the floating double taper (DT), which has a long belly or middle section that tapers at both ends and thus is reversible, one end for the other. A weight forward (WF) and shooting taper (ST) have a smaller diameter and lighter weight running line portion than the heads, which carry lures under the water.

There are other weight forward tapers for shooting rockets, bass bugs, saltwater, and steelhead lures.

Fly fishing reels are used to store line and for playing a fish by setting the drag. Drag is friction brake resistance applied to a line against which a fish must work when being played. The drag helps tire out a fish so it can be caught quicker. As the fish tires, the runs are shorter and shorter. Give the fish a break! Don't use a telephone pole and a hawser to haul in a brookie! If you're going after big fish, learn to set the drag on the reel. I generally found fly-fishermen set the drag too tightly, forgetting the weight of the line, the friction through the guides, and the diminishing circumference of the line on the reel. They all add to the drag. Pull the line from the reel, squeezing it between your lips until it slips when setting the drag. It's a good gauge to test the resistance.

Backing line refers to a single diameter line that is used to fill the reel, so the casting line takes up the larger diameter of the reel. The backing also serves to foster the fisherman's dream of catching such a whopper that strips out all the casting line. The reserve is needed for a hard-running trophy fish that takes the line three miles (Ahem! Mild exaggeration!) upstream rather than have the fisherman run alongside the fish on the bank to keep up with it. The stuff of dreams.

When I fly-fish, I carry the reel in my pocket. I like to have the rod as light as possible, and don't need it as a casting counterbalance or any such thing. I use the guides to keep the rod facing forward.

To summarize, the equipment so far consists of a rod, a reel, and a casting line. The next thing to be added to the casting line is a tapered "leader."

A leader is a tapered piece of monofilament or a newer type of line and may or may not have color added. Not only does the leader lengthen the taper of the fly line, but it is to keep as much of the connection of the line to the fisherman invisible to the fish.

Generally speaking, the leader is about seven and a half feet long and tapers down to a graded tensile strength end, usually a 3X. A 3X is stronger than a 1X and not as strong as a 7X. Tensile strength means how much longitudinal stress in pounds per square inch a line can take before it breaks. The preferred leader is knotless, which tells you there is also a leader that is tied together in decreasingly sized sections to make the taper.

The next piece of equipment is added to the end of the leader, and it is called the tippet (spelled the same as a rod tippet and meaning the top or end). I call it the "mystery connection" between the fly and the fisherman. In no way do you want the fish to know there is a connection between the fly and the person fishing. It is the last piece of the fly line to touch the water. A super-properly cast fly will see the fly land on the water followed by a "hump" in the tippet; then, the hump gradually eases onto the water. It lands "softly," or mysteriously, which means it doesn't scare the fish away with a splash. This is a truly mastered cast and a beauty to behold. It's supposed to make the fish think that yummy tidbit of a fly just landed right out of thin air by magic—just as Nature intended.

The tippet is also rated for tensile strength, which should be determined against and less than the leader's breaking point, of course. The higher number meaning the lower the breaking point, such as 3X or 5X or 7X, and are bought in small spools. Two improved clinch knots generally are used to tie the ends of the leader and the tippet together. One practice is to use a heavier leader to accommodate a smaller-X tippet. To review, a 3X tippet tied to a 5X leader is backward. The higher x-number, the thinner the leader.

The tippet is added on to the leader. It is done this way because as the tippet is used up by having the knot portion cut away, making it shorter every time a fly is cut off and a new one tied on. Replacing the shortened tippet is more practical than replacing the entire leader. If you're wondering whether the tippet has become too short and should be replaced—replace the tippet.

The Cast Line

The spectacular world of fly-fishing starts with properly casting an artificial fly.

From that, every other aspect of this alluring sport is open. A bonus will be self-discovery.

As you become familiar with the art and science of fly-fishing, you will learn more and more about yourself. For example, your temperament and personality will have to adjust to fly-fishing. It doesn't work the other way around.

FLY FISHING SAFETY RULE
NEVER TO BE BROKEN:

ALWAYS WEAR EYE PROTECTION

An avid fly fisherman, I have restricted my 35 years of teaching to just the cast. I have always felt it is that important. I needed only one lesson with a fisherman to get the student on the way. There are a myriad of teachers and books that more than—to a greater or lesser degree—adequately and expertly cover all the gazillion other aspects of fly fishing in more detail and more precisely than anyone can combine in one book, excluding encyclopedias. All of them are useless if one hasn't mastered the art of casting a fly.

The art of casting the fly line has stopped too many sportsmen from entering the most pleasurable world of fly-fishing. Many did not find a competent teacher. Others were stopped by what seemed an insurmountable mystery in making the cast. Some were plain impatient. Some were disappointed and dejected because they had spent hundreds of dollars on casting lessons and still were unable to make a decent cast. And other fishermen cannot deny the urge to fly-fish and do so with "what-the-heck" bad casts, beat the water to a froth, and yes, they catch fish. They'd rather do it badly than not do it at all. I can't fault these fishermen, but I'd be happy to teach them how to fly cast.

Many fly fishermen run into trouble on their casts because they do not understand—using a fancy word—the "dynamics" of the cast line. It also makes it exceedingly difficult for them to learn how to correct bad casts. I'm particularly speaking about the bad cast that reverses power too quickly that causes it to snap like a whip that breaks off the fly. A bad cast is one that reverses direction too late and allows the end of the line to make a lazy-eight and become what is called a wind knot. Or, a bad cast can start out making a wind knot, falter, get caught in reversed direction balling the line to make what is called a bird's nest. More often, with a bad cast, the fisherman must stop to crank up the line and begin the cast all over again.

This treatise will enable anyone to understand the essence of fly-casting. Then, in actual practice in a truly short time, you can be out on your front lawn making decent casts. Assuming you want to do this, your progress will depend on self-discovery dealing mainly with patience and learning to be kind to yourself.

Fly-casting is a skill. As with any sport—tennis, skiing, sailing—a skill cannot be acquired all at once. A skill, by its definition, is an accretion. It is the acquiring of a skill by adding one layer of correct experience on top of the other layers of correct experience. It is a learned power assimilated bit by bit by bit that enables one to do something competently most of the time. Practice makes perfect, yes, but to learn the art, one must practice correctly! The adage is there is no right way to do the wrong thing.

As the skill of pencil drawing comes with the reduction of error, so it is with the skill of casting with a fly rod.

A professional can perform a skill repeatedly with minimal errors. Human ingenuity enables us to do this.

In bait casting or spin fishing, the weight of the lure can carry out a very light monofilament line. Here, the energy put into casting the lure is the energy that takes out the line. The distance the lure goes depends on the amount of energy that is put into it, like how far and fast one can throw a baseball.

In fly-fishing, it is the line that takes out the lure or artificial fly. The concept is based on the fact that there is no more effective way to cast an almost weightless mere wisp of a fly. So, it is in the line where we put the energy needed to send the artificial fly some distance.

The energy put into a thrown baseball goes out entirely in and within the baseball. There isn't a bit of energy kept in reserve. When the energy put into the baseball is used up, it is gone, and the ball falls to the ground.

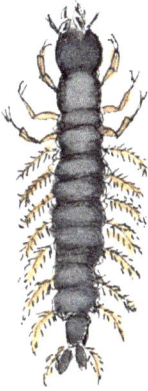

8. DOBSON FLY – LARVA

9. DOBSON FLY – ADULT FEMALE

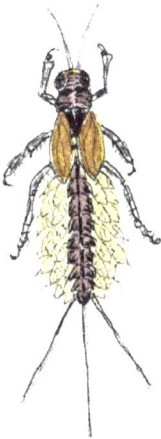

10. MAYFLY – NYMPH

11. MAYFLY – ADULT

First, a definition. Some, in fly-casting, loosely use the term "loop" in a fly-line. A loop pretty much is a circle. That's not exactly what is meant. The reference is to an "arc," a "semi-circle," a "half-circle." The arc is what the fly-line forms when it is cast. For the ease of it, I'll use the terms—loop, arc, semi-circle—interchangeably.

In casting a fly-line, the energy is put into the line, let's say, a bit at a time. The energy put into the line starts as an arc and is all used up when the arc straightens out. The energy in the fly-line is put to work a bit at a time as it flies through the air until it gets to the end. This is what allows twenty, thirty, forty, or more feet of line to fly.

When the energy is used up in a baseball, it falls to the ground, perhaps rolls a bit, and then stops. If we wanted to re-energize the baseball, we could throw it towards a batter who can whack it with a baseball bat and send it flying again.

Now, suppose instead of a baseball, we use a ball of yarn. If we hold onto the end of the yarn and throw the ball of yarn as hard as we're able, the ball of yarn would unwind and get smaller and smaller as it went further and further. Finally, it would reach its end, and the ball of yarn would be no more, and the yarn would collapse to the ground.

How does a fly-line fly? It doesn't use up its energy the same as a baseball. But energy is imparted to the fly-line. How does the fly-line use the energy put into it? A fly-line doesn't use up its energy all at once, or it would fall in a heap. So? How does a fly-line fly?

In fly-fishing, the energy generated by the fly-fisherman using the fly rod and the fly line is made to fly by the energy imparted when the loop is created.

The energy in the loop is released by impulse. The definition of an impulse is "the act of driving onward with sudden force." Said another way, it is an impelling action or force, driving onward or inducing motion. This is not necessarily to be confused with impulsive buying, but you're in the ballpark. My definition of impulse is a wave of force transmitted through a fly-line. The energy, or wave of force carried by the loop, travels incrementally down the line toward the end. This is somewhat like, but not quite the force one sees in an ocean wave as it moves toward the shore in an arc, which expires from the top of the arc inward as it crashes onto the beach. In other words, the arc is a short-lived storage battery for the energy created by the cast, which is released by impulse.

What makes a fly-line fly? **A fly-line flies by kinetic impulse.** Kinetic impulse energy is imparted and generated from and by the fisherman's hold on the handle up to the tip of the rod, and down the line in the form of a loop to its very end. It may be aided and abetted by a supplementary, complimentary tug on the line by the fisherman.

In a fly-line, it will continue to fly until the impulse energy in the form of a loop is used up until the last bit, and then it will collapse to the ground.

I found students understood better how a fly-line worked when I visualized for them kinetic impulse power. In a broad, loose generalization. I explained first that when a baseball is thrown, it has no work to do in and of itself. Impulse power does work by the path it travels and by what it is doing. The work it does is make the fly-line fly.

The broadest visualization of impulse power at work involves a hill, a bowling ball, and a long, flexible tube slightly larger than the diameter of the bowling ball made of say, plastic.

If we pulled the long plastic tube up a hill and anchored the end at the top of the hill, we will have kinetic impulse power at work the moment we shove the bowling ball into that opening, and it starts rolling down inside the tube on the other side of the hill because of gravity. We can find objections with this, but just accept the fact that the bowling ball is captured impulse power. (Gravity is making the ball roll down the hill where the fly-caster generates impulse power.) It does work by opening the plastic tube as it forms a loop in the tube as it rolls and pulls the other end of the tube that is behind us up the hill. Soon, that end passes us at the peak of the hill and starts down alongside the tube. As the hill levels out the bowling ball gets closer and closer to the end of the tube and then pops out, runs out of energy, and stops. The empty tube runs straight down the hill.

It would be difficult to visualize a bowling ball going down a hollow center of a thin fly-line, but essentially the bowling ball represents the impulse power that makes a fly line fly.

Primarily, it is understood, and enough energy must be imparted so the impulse will travel to the end of the line. Should the impulse not reach the end of the line, very simply, the line will not fly. The line will collapse on top of itself. There will be no fishing! So, be a little aggressive if you must, and perform as if you know what you're doing and put all the energy the line needs to get up into the air.

If we want to re-energize the fly line, we must give it another **tug** to send it flying but in the opposite direction. The kinetic impulse energy put into the fly-line travels down the line a bit at a time in the form of a loop!

Only when the loop has run out can the line be re-energized. When a line that already has energy in it and is flying has additional energy put into it, one energy conflicts with the other, and one is left holding a mess.

We know the energy has run out of the line when the loop that has powered it is gone, and the line is straight. The only energy available is gravity, and that makes the line fall to the ground.

The reason for this is because one cannot have the energy going in one direction have it confront the energy going in the opposite direction. It would be like putting two steam engines head to head under full power. Either the wheels would spin, or the engines would crush into one another. This is the reason one must wait until the line is straight, indicating all the energy is out of the line and will not conflict with the tug to re-energize the line. If there is the slightest conflict in out-going and in-coming energy, the result is a bad cast.

As long as there is a loop in a fly-line, it can perform work, some of it unintentional work such as making wind knots, birds' nests, changing direction, or even hitting the fly-fisherman. For now, accept the fact that a loop can only do one thing at a time. For example, if the fly-fisherman tried to re-energize a loop, all sorts of crazy things happen. First and foremost, it makes for a terrible cast.

To repeat, one must wait for the energy in a fly-line to dissipate before it can be re-energized. (P.S. There is an exception to this, but it's a specialized occasion we'll get to later, known as "turning a corner" or "wiggle cast," which has to do with adding an impulse but it does not go counter but complements the original impulse.) We know the energy is all gone when the loop has run out, and the line is straight. How do we know when this happens? **We watch the line**.

The essential, critical part of fly-casting is determining when the fly-line is straight when the energy has been dissipated. **If there is a loop, energy exists.** Said another way, a loop represents energy working the line.

This is so vital I cannot emphasize it enough. Kindly just accept this as a fact for now until we've done a little more house-cleaning, and then we'll get back to it.

And, so, it is in controlling the energy in the line that enables us to fly-cast effectively.

In any case, the object is to have a fish strike at the lure, get caught on the hook, and for the angler to retrieve the line to capture the fish. In a word, fishing.

Before we get into line control, we should understand we are entered full blast into the world of physics. In this world is energy. If you can understand how energy works and its application, you can understand what happens in fly casting and that knowledge will enable you to make a fly line do your bidding. Applying your capacity to the physics will enable you to master casting the fly. It's that simple.

Before we get to the dynamics, I cannot again emphasize enough that fly fishing is a matter of making a constant adjustment to some aspect that affects the fly fisherman at his pleasure. Your adaptability to adjusting some aspect of fly fishing—whether it's dealing with equipment, weather, wind, time of day, or even your temperament—will determine your enjoyment satisfaction level. Nothing can be taken for granted; nothing is certain. The only thing cast in brass is that you must be prepared to be adaptable.

Here's the skinny on fly casting.

Kinetic energy is the name given to motion energy. Think of energy as the ability to do work. It is the energy in a moving object. A speeding automobile, a thrown football, a cast fly line are examples of objects that are using up kinetic energy. In the simplest of terms, kinetic energy may be thought of as moving energy or energy on the move. It is a finite amount of energy captured in a physical object. For example, an impulse put into a fly-line. As the object moves, it expends the energy that was put into it. Eventually, it will run out of energy and stop like a watch that has run down or like a free-flying arrow that falls to the ground.

The other kind of energy is potential energy. It is energy **potentially** ready to be put to work. It is energy standing at rest. It is energy waiting to be used. In effect, energy has been put into an object, and that object is waiting to be used. When that "at rest" energy is put into use, it changes into kinetic or moving action. A form of potential energy would be the heavy weights in a grandfather clock, which use gravity to keep the clock works going once the pendulum is put into motion. Winding up the weights uses kinetic energy, which will be used to store potential energy until they are released to the force of gravity, and their weight is used to make the clock run. Eventually, the weights reach the limits of their cords and just hang suspended. Resting this way, they are neither kinetic nor potential energy. They are just hanging weights. Their status is changed when they are rewound (kinetic energy) and raised to the top (potential energy) where their weight may be used to affect the clock's movement.

Per the formula for kinetic energy $E_k = mv^2/2$ (Kinetic energy equals mass times its velocity squared divided by 2) the velocity of a cast line increases with the decrease in mass, which primarily allows a tapered fly line to fly. Basically, what that says is the thinner a line gets (because the resistance is less, for one thing), the faster it moves. The principle is as the initial energy decreases in a cast line, it needs less energy to move the portion of the line that is diminishing or tapered. That is one reason a little bit of energy at the rod goes such a long way down the line.

13. MOTH – LARVA, LEAF CASE

14. MOTH – ADULT

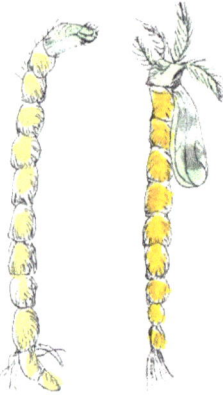

12. MIDGE – LARVA, PUPA, ADULT

15A. GIANT STONEFLY

15. STONEFLY – ADULT

An object that has had energy put into it and is being used immediately is kinetic energy, like the energy put into a thrown baseball.

Potential energy loosely may be defined as matter that has had energy put into it and is waiting to be used. One form of kinetic energy is to stretch rubber bands on a slingshot. Once the rubber bands have been pulled back and are waiting to be released, they have potential energy. When a fly rod has been bent, either forward or backward, it has potential energy that is waiting to be turned into kinetic energy the moment it can move forward or backward. In fishing jargon, it's called "loading the rod," just as one would "load" a slingshot. A fly rod becomes loaded when the line is cast either forward or backward, and the weight of the line makes the rod bend. In effect, the loaded rod acts as the stretched rubber bands on a slingshot. It is not waiting to propel a missile, however, but rather to put its energy into the fly-line.

This kinetic-potential-kinetic energy series is what happens when fly casting.

Casting a fly line is a special situation. It can be explained as follows in a very rudimentary way.

A person standing on one side of the stream wishes to put a near weightless fly-fishing lure on the other side of the stream. Let's say there are three ways of doing it.

The first way would be for the person to pick up the lure attached to one end of a fly line, and, allowing the line to uncoil on the bank, walks the lure pulling the end of the line over to the other bank and placing the lure close to the shore. Then, the person would walk back to the other side, pick up the other end of the line and wait for a fish to strike the lure. You're shaking your head and smirking, and I don't blame you.

A second way could be if the fly was attached to the end of a fly line, and then the fly line and lure were tied to a rock. Then, the rock would be hurled across the water to the other side, pulling the line behind it. Here, the energy is put into the rock, and the rock pulls the line behind it (just like spin casting). The fly would not appear natural, of course, and the splash would scare the fins off a fish. Pulling the rock and the lure back just won't work to attract a fish, especially if it's a dry fly.

The closest one can get to fly-casting would be to wind up the fly-line into a ball, like a ball of yarn, hold on to the end, and throw the ball of line across the river. It certainly would work because it would land the fly on the other bank. However, it would be a very impractical way of fishing because it would mean winding and throwing and winding and throwing. There is an easier way.

The most practical way to get a lure to the other bank would be to use a fly-line, which, with a fly rod can be easily cast and placed anywhere near the bank with accuracy and with naturalness if one knew how to cast a fly. How clever is that!

There is a price to pay to be able to do this.

The price is to take the time to learn the remarkably simple trick of doing it. Precisely what that art or trick may be is difficult to understand unless it is dissected, taken apart one step at a time to reveal exactly what is going on. Once you understand it, you'll know what you must do. I want to show you this.

All three ways to get the lure on the other side of the river use energy—kinetic energy because it is moving—but in different forms. Above, the first method is walking energy, the second is hurling energy, and the third way with a fly line is a special energy that is "impulse energy," which takes the form of a loop in the fly-line. Now, hold this thought of "impulse energy" because there are some other basics that must be covered before we show how this can put a fly on the other side of the river.

When a fly line is cast, it uses kinetic energy in a rolling fashion (the bit by bit, as I mentioned earlier). Now, that is not exactly, perfectly true, an engineer would say, but accept it for now.

A rudimentary example of rolling action would be if the line were wound around a wheel. If we took the loose end of the line and pulled the line off the wheel, the wheel would turn because we are using energy to unwind the line until we ran out of line. Eventually, the wheel would stop turning. The difference between this and fly casting is that the power of the line is not rolled onto the wheel, but instead of a wheel, the power that is put into the line is continually rolling down the line by impulse in the form of an arc-loop, if you will. The loop takes the form of an arc—like the letter "C," which "rolls" until it comes to the end of the line.

The critical point to note is that the kinetic energy is the impulse that makes the loop of the line that runs down the line from the tip of the fishing rod to the end of the line. The line is unwinding down, going toward the bottom of the loop (which goes back to the tip of the rod), and at the same time winding up at the top (which goes toward the end of the line). Another way of saying this is that the fly line at the bottom of the loop gets longer (because the impulse is traveling down the line away from the tip), and the fly line at the top of the loop gets shorter. A visual of this would be to put the palms of your hands facing each other with your fingertips pointing toward the wrists and have them pass one over and one under the other in opposite directions. If a loop connected your palms, we would almost have the dynamics of a flying line.

This is the closest example of visualizing how the energy put into a fly line allows it to be cast. Let us break this down into more straightforward explanations.

The two requirements are that the energy (impulse) is shoved down the line in the form of a loop and that the line is flexible enough to form the loop, which gets longer on the bottom as it rolls down toward the tip of the line on the top. What is the reason for these requirements?

Let's just say the art of fly casting was created by a coachman sitting on the bank of a stream in Scotland. He had his whip beside him. He was so adept at the use of the whip he could split a leaf in half on the water. Or, he could use it to flick the hind end of a horse he was driving. He understood that the impulse energy of the unrolling loop of a tapered whip worked very well because as the plait of the whip diminished—or tapered, as explained earlier—it increased in speed and allowed him—by snapping the whip at the exact right instant—just before the loop reached the end (or straightened out!), to make a "Crack!", as it flicked the horse. This served to signal the animal. The coachman wouldn't know it in the year 1620, but that "Sn-a-a-a-p" was the sound that came from breaking the sound barrier. The tip of the whip had to travel the speed of sound to catch up to itself when the coachman reversed its direction from going downwards to suddenly being snapped upwards. (At the ice-skating show, remember how blooming fast the last skater had to zip around creating a vacuum behind her to catch up to the line? Same thing, but speed of sound FASTER!) Nature abhors a vacuum, so when the tip went racing around to catch up to itself, it created a vacuum with the air rushing in to fill the void; it created the explosive sound. To make the whip crack, it required exact timing, which didn't take long for the coachman to learn to do.

This is the same as boys in a locker room snapping a towel to raise a welt on an unsuspecting victim. They would roll a towel into a "rat's tail" (fat on one end, thin on the other) and crack the thin end against a bare leg. With the heavy end of the towel in one hand and the thin end in the other, the action was to whip the thin end forward, which made the towel form a loop, releasing the thin end just as the heavy end was yanked backward to make the tip snap. The thin end would shoot forward, then whip around on itself faster than the speed of sound precisely aimed to strike the leg as it did so and make a loud crack. It requires exact timing.

The tiny end whips around so fast it injures the skin, precisely as a "cat o' nine tails," which used the same reversal action, that would cause it to flay the skin of its victim. The tip of the rat's tail would create a vacuum in which the air—rushing in to fill it—breaks the sound barrier. Lightning causes the same effect and produces thunder. These same heavy-handed physics, involved in making a whip crack, are used to make a stock whip (popular in Australia)—(this usually has about a two-foot wooden handle to which the plaited leather is attached)— also "ca-rack" like a rifle shot. But, the heavy-handed jerking of the whip or bull or stock whip, which requires exact timing—is discarded and for fly-fishing for casting a smoother, longer, more flowing, timed toss and retrieve.

This fast movement forward and fast jerking back is precisely what we do not want to do when we are fly casting.

The coachman was only one good hard thought away from developing the fly rod and fly line. His whip, which was tapered, was all one piece of plaited leather, with a "cracker"—a folded short piece of leather—at the end. The single, tapered piece was excellent as a basis for the fly rod, but what was needed was an adjustment so the fishing line could be let out and taken in. In a manner, ferrules—the metal tubes that slide into one another to join two sections of the fly rod—and snake guides (which held the line close to the rod) were added to a rod-shaped—tapered—like a whip, and the fly rod was born.

The fly fisherman is not driving cattle using a stock whip to make loud sounds like rifle shots to drive the animals. He is a gentle, subtle stalker of the wary trout.

The art of making the cast is a lot gentler, a lot smoother, a lot less frenetic.

In the simplest way, here are the physics involved with making a cast.

Now, if I picked up one end of a fly line that was stretched out behind me and I started walking, the entire fly line would follow me as I kept moving. This is what settlers did crossing the plains. They dragged a long rope behind the last wagon that made a perfectly straight line and was used as a guide to making sure they didn't travel in a circle.

As a hypothetical, suppose I was dragging a rope, and then I decided I should change something. Suppose I let my hand that was holding the end of the line down by the side of my leg go behind me by about a foot, and then gave this end of the line a good, hard yank forward suddenly stopping my hand when it got back to my side.

What happens is the line—the entire line—moves, and then the part closest to my hand shoots ahead of me. It shoots ahead, but because I'm holding on to the end, the only way it can use the energy is to form a loop. It shoots ahead almost precisely the length of the distance I moved my hand from back to front. So, if I yanked my hand ahead by one foot, the line would skootch in front of me by one foot.

16. LARGE STONEFLY – NYMPH

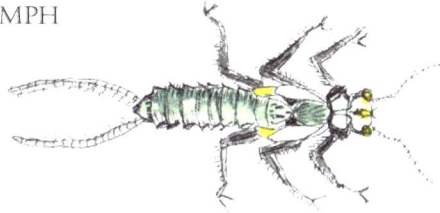

17. PERLA SPRING STONEFLY – NYMPH

18. EARLY SPRING STONEFLY –
    NYMPH

19. EARLY SPRING
    STONEFLY – ADULT

20. WHITETAIL – ADULT

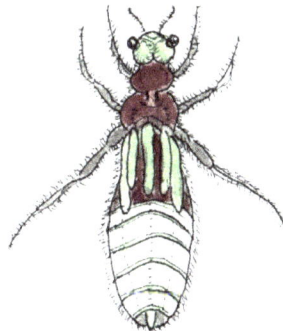

21. WHITETAIL – NYMPH

The vital thing to notice here is that the entire line moved up that same one foot! The tail end of the line moved the same distance as the head of the line.

Simply, I energized the entire line by yanking it that one foot.

The next important fact to notice is how did that line manage to move that foot in front of me?

It did so in the only way it could by impulse, that is to form a loop or make an arc from my hand—which held the end—to the ground where it pulled the line until it ran out of energy.

By continuing to walk, I would capture—or catch up to—the line that went ahead, and by yanking it forward again, I could move the line up again. The line would progress by "jerks" as we suddenly increased the amount of energy we put into it.

Now comes a highly interesting explanation.

Suppose instead of dragging the line behind me on the ground; I could some-how float the line in the air behind me at, say, ear level, and continue to drag it behind me. Picture that—the line running out in a straight line behind me float-ing about five feet above the ground. Now, with that magic, if I happened to yank the line forward as I did when I had to contend with the friction of the ground, the line would shoot ahead of me by also forming a loop in front of me for the line to move ahead of me. This time, instead of the loop forming in front of my shoe, it forms in front and above my head. That loop then flies forward to increase in distance from where I held it at my ear and diminishes in length behind me and rolls out in front of me! It must do this because of kinetic energy, and because the line does not stretch. It would be as if the end of the line was pushing the line ahead of it until it came up to the loop and then back to my hand. The loop would continue to move forward because of the initial yank or energy I put into the line. Remember, there is no friction from the ground to contend with, but the much-reduced friction of going through the air with only gravity against it. Given enough energy, the loop would run out when it got to the end of the line. When the loop reaches the end, the entire line is straightened out lying on this magic ear level, except it is no longer behind me but in front of me! How wonderful is that!

Okay. For the next exercise, let's have you make a perfect cast the first time you try with a fly-fishing rod.

Here's how you can do it. I guarantee you it will work.

Let's say you are looking at the figure nine on a clock face and holding a fly rod with the tip over your shoulder behind you pointed at, say, the numeral three on a clock. Let's say we have a length of fly line that goes straight out behind you from the tip of the rod, down to the ground for whatever length of line, but just for this exercise, let's say it's twenty-five feet long. Now, just to add some drama, you are going to hold on to the handle of the rod and wade out to exact midstream with the line still straight out behind you. Now, let's say we are going to have you capture the line under your hand by the handle so it would not slip out. Next, using enough energy, yank the rod tip forward in a straight line in an arc past the clock face numbers two, one, twelve, eleven, ten, and even down to the eight if you wish. What happens to the line? Whenever you stop the rod, the line forms a loop that continues to move forward toward the opposite bank and finally will run out of energy and lands on the water, AND the line will land in a straight line! Tah-Rah! You have made a cast! Surprisingly good one, too.

Now, play along with me, and let's say, you turn around to the opposite bank while you're still standing in the middle of the stream, and with **the line laying in a straight line behind you,** you repeat your action with the rod tip scribing a straight line. What happens? Why you make another perfect cast to the other bank! Imagine that? Now, if we can eliminate the line landing after every cast, we could be flying the line! Or, fly-casting. Really. Cast, let the fly land; turn around to face the other bank, cast, and let the fly land. In effect, you are fly-casting, but not in a very efficient, subtle, or continuous way. There must be a way to keep the line flying in the air forward and backward until we want the fly to land in a particular place. Yes, of course, there is such a method.

Now you knew this was all too good to be true. Right you are because here's the kicker. How do we get to fly the line from one side of the bank to the other without letting it land first?

You have just anchored the first principle in fly-casting. **The entire flying line must be straight before you can reverse its direction.** It cannot have the slightest bit of a loop above or below the line. Another way of saying it is that there cannot be even the last little bit of the loop remaining. The loop as it winds down may look like the handle of a cane, either facing up or facing down.

If you pulled the line when it looked like the handle of the cane (the loop) facing upwards, you were too early.

If you activated the line when it looked like the handle of the cane (the loop) was facing downwards very simply, it means you are late.

If the line is activated in either case—cane handle up or down—the result could be knots, nests, and nothing casts simply because the line was not straight when you tugged it in the opposite direction.

Review this: the essential principle is that the line must be straight before we add any energy.

It only takes another instant of thought to realize that if we were able to give the end, I am holding in my hand a yank in the backward direction it would do the same thing in the backward direction until it, too, straightened out to be exactly as it was in the beginning.

This yanking the line forward, making a loop, the loop moving down the length of the line until it got to the end and straightened out to the end of the line, is the cast! I mean, this is what the fly fisherman does when he allows the line to collapse to let the fly land on the water!

That is flying the line! That is casting!

So? Where does the difficulty come in? What was just described is too simple. That is precisely the point I'm making. What we have to come up with is a method to have the line stretched out straight behind us (or in front of us), so we could tug at the line, and have it straighten out before us, allow the energy to dissipate, and let the fly land. Fly-casting! That's it! Except for one point: In doing what we just described, we're not false casting the line. It's a "false" cast because a "true" cast lets the fly land, but in this case, we do not allow the cast to land. We continue to keep the line flying in the air both in front and behind us. We want to keep the line going back and forth. So, no problem. Let's do it.

Are there caveats? Conditions under which this must be done if it is to be continuous?

Of course. It's what confuses fly casters and makes them think there's some mystery they are unable to solve, which is not so. Here, this very point is the heart and the art of fly-casting.

We are at the point that has made ladies and gentlemen cry.

This point where the fly line changes direction while it is in the air!

The fly line is flying behind us, and suddenly, we must make it change its direction and fly in front of us.

Why is this point so crucial? I have already explained the principles involved.

One cannot have two steam engines pushing in opposite directions.

One cannot say, "Stop! Go ahead!" in the same sentence. If I heard someone say that to me, I would say, "Make up your mind!"

The law of the fly-line says, "Don't try to make me double in brass. Either I'm going backward, or forward, but I can't, absolutely, do both."

Yes, you understand what that says, but what does it mean?

It means if you are flying the line backward—behind you—you must wait until it has stopped going backward before you try to make it go forward.

How does one know when the line has stopped going backward? When the loop traveling down the line comes to the end of the line and is straight!

The trick here is to determine when the line has stopped going backward. The line has stopped going back when the energy has been used up. Just as a thrown baseball stops when the energy is used up, the energy in a fly line is used up when the energy in the loop is used up, and the loop straightens out. At that moment, there is no more energy in the line. There is no backward energy, no forward energy. If the line can use up its energy by going straight, if nothing else is done to the line, it will collapse to the ground because of gravity.

Now, are you aware that is precisely what a fly fisherman does when he wants to present his fly to the water and allows the line and the fly to use up its energy and land on the water? He allows the line to collapse. It is a perfectly legitimate cast.

But the problem is what if the fisherman wants to make some false casts—meaning to keep the line in the air, say, to dry off a fly or wants to change the direction of the line. What is the problem?

The problem is determining **the exact moment** the energy in the line—meaning the loop, as we've said before—has been used up. Yes, the loop ends, and the line becomes straight!

This is somewhat like skeet shooting. The gun is not aimed at where the clay pigeon is, but where the clay pigeon will be! That is **anticipating** the action.

The problem here depends on three factors solely and totally within the fly caster.

Those three factors are:

- At what point the fisherman sees the loop coming to an end.
- At precisely what point before the unrolling line reaches its end must the fisherman apply force in the other direction.
- Which is the point of <u>anticipation</u> when the fisherman has determined that by the time he applies the tug in the other direction, the line will be precisely straight.

In other words, the fisherman sees the loop in the line about to end. It may be two feet away, or it may be a foot away from ending.

The knack, the art is for the fisherman to guess how soon before the loop ends must he start his reverse tug so that by the time he has tugged the line in the opposite direction, the line is precisely straight.

The answer is this moment of anticipation must come with practice and adjustments. Not every case will be the same. Some will be faster, some slower—remember your uniqueness. The wind may come up. The rain may affect the line. So, the trick is to practice and get close to perfect timing when practice conditions are all ideal. When you have made the line fly back and forth several times in a row, you know you have gauged your anticipation and timing on both forward and backward casts very well, and have opened the door to this wonderful sport. Pat yourself on the back! You deserve it!

What happens if the fisherman anticipates and tugs too early or too late?

If the fisherman tugs too early, the end of the fly line will snap like a whip and break off the fly, or tie a knot in the line, or creates a tangled ball of the line that is called a bird's nest.

If the fisherman tugs too late, the force of gravity will take over, the line will collapse striking the ground or the water, tie a wind knot, create a bird's nest, or will shoot wildly forward possibly wrapping itself around or striking the fisherman.

The great danger here is if the line shoots unidirectionally forward, strikes the head of the fisherman, wraps itself around the fisherman's head that will be very lucky if the fly at the end of the line does not strike the fisherman's eyeglasses. The moment you determine your cast is not proper, stop the action! Let the line collapse and start over. No one is keeping score. No meter is running. The time is all yours. Just don't get discouraged. Next time you'll do it correctly.

Let's get into reaction time a bit. We're talking about your reaction time. How fast or how slow does it take you to perform a function from the instant you get the message to initiating action to do it. Whatever it is, you adjust to it. It's your reaction time that's important, not anyone else's! Don't try to change it! Just know it!

This reaction time is super-critical at automobile drag races where two competitors are signaled when they may leave the starting gate with signals from "Christmas tree lights." There may be six perpendicular traffic lights with the top light showing red, the next two or three yellow, and the last one green, or some such combination. When the starter pushes the button to begin the race, the lights run down from one to another in a sporadic fashion. Going out of the gate before the green light disqualifies the driver. The edge on this type of start depends on which driver has the fastest anticipation/reaction time: that fraction of a second when the light turns green, and he stomps on the gas and leaves the gate. Here the difference between winning and losing is fractions of a split second. The difference is which driver is the first to take his foot off the brake and jam the gas to the floor with the other foot to be a millimeter of a second first out of the starting gate. It is **anticipating** when the light will be green and reacting to it at the precise split second.

Fly-fishing requires no such competition. It is somewhat less critical, but critical it is. You are required to anticipate the moment BEFORE the line straightens out, and when you move the fly rod in the opposite direction.

If the caster misjudges and yanks too quickly, there is a clash of forces—the ending energy of the cast line and the new energy of the moving fly rod—and the line goes bad. If the caster yanks too late, the line drops down too much and causes re-energizing problems.

The fly fisherman may consider he has a Christmas tree lights starter, too, but the great thing is that it is not a sporadic run of the lights. Because the timing is evenly spaced for the fisherman, he can gauge the timing of just how far from the end the loop may be before he pulls the line to make both actions coincide! That is where the art comes in.

I'll call it the **art of anticipating and coordinating**.

It means the fly caster must anticipate how far ahead of the line straightening out must he coordinate the pull of the line so that the tug comes at the exact point when the line is straight. No machine can teach you this. No muscle memory can help. You must teach yourself exactly how much time you need to react to what you determine your fly line is going to be a straight line.

This represents the real difficulty in casting a fly line. Overcoming this difficulty rests in the fly-caster—how close attention is paid, and how hard one is willing to work.

This difficulty—believe it or not—is compounded by other conditions. These conditions include how much line is out; how energized is the line; how hard if at all, the wind is blowing.

Making the adjustment or adjustments is the reason only you can teach yourself how to fly-cast.

Let us continue coordinating the pull of the rod and the line straightening out. Once the fly fisherman learns how long or short to wait before he pulls forward, it will be almost metronomic. He soon can say—as the loop moves down the line—wait! Wait! Wait! Now! and learn the timing to make perfect casts every time that needs no adjustment.

So, the answer is for the caster to be aware of how fast or slow is his or her reaction time.

Okay, let's move forward. How can the beginning fly fisherman recognize when the line is about to straighten out?

First, watch someone fly fishing. This is a vital exercise. Keep a sharp eye on the line and say, "Now!" when you think the line is coming to its end. As I was

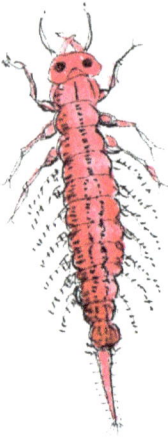

22. ALDERLY – LARVA

23. ALDERLY – ADULT

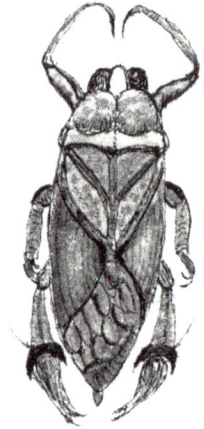

24. ELECTRIC
LIGHT BUG

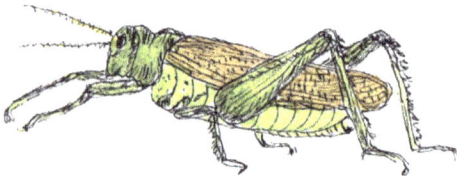

25. GRASSHOPPER

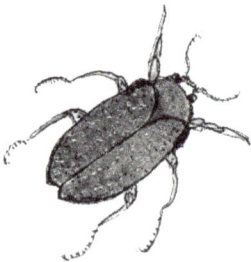

26. HORSEFLY

27. WATER PENNY

false casting, first, I would have the student identify the loop as it rolled down toward the end of the line. Next, I would have the student tap me just when the loop was about to end.

Next was more difficult. I had to let the student know that his or her rate of anticipation may or may not be different than mine. But I could tell if the student was in the ballpark. A student with an acute sense of anticipation would tap me when the loop was a mere 12 inches from straightening out. Generally, the students would tap me when the loop was about 18 inches from straightening out. I felt this was a good point at which that student should tug the line in the opposite direction. Often, the student got the anticipation spot on and made very successful casts. For these students, I would suggest they could understand. If one had to be a tad early or a tad late on the tug, it was better to be a tad early. (The theatre admonition is, "If you ain't early, you're late!)

The reason for that is because the fly caster can use the bit of energy remaining in the loop of the line to use less of his energy to change the direction of the line. In tennis, it takes a lot more energy to hit back a softly hit ball. The reason for that is because the tennis player must generate ALL the energy need to whack the ball back. Whereas, if the ball is hit hard to the receiver, he uses the energy in the ball to hit the ball back harder than without it. Essentially what happens is that a hard-hit ball pushes deeply against the strings of the racket—like the rubber bands being pulled back on a slingshot—and adds to the speed of the ball flying off the racket. Another example would be a batter would not hit a baseball as far if he hits a baseball just hanging on a string in front of him as he would when the ball is thrown at him at 100 miles an hour. This is exactly what happens when the fisherman loads the rod as he tugs the line to change direction. So, a tad bit ahead is okay; a tad bit too much, and the fly is snapped off, so approach this point carefully.

With those students that had difficulty coordinating the anticipation and the tug, I would say, "Too late!" or "Too early!" or "Spot on!" After ten or so false casts, they were able to pick up the exact moment on a forward or backward cast to anticipate when to tug the line before the loop reached the end with no problem.

Then, some students had a problem discerning when the loop was going to end, and the line straightens out. I devised a method to make it quite easy and safe for them to see the action in slow motion.

This is what I devised.

4

The Ribbon Method

Using the student's fly rod without line or reel, I tied about twelve feet of half-inch ribbon to the guide on the tip.

My instructions were simple: **As the tip of the rod goes, so goes the ribbon.**

I showed them how to fly the ribbon, make it go in circles, in straight lines, in front and behind them, go back and forth, write their names, and, can you believe? Have them make the motion of a cast and anticipate when the loop was going to straighten out at the end of the line! You can do the same thing without further instructions!

It will bring you into the ballpark of fly-casting. It's close, but not the same. It will make it easier for you to follow the loop in the ribbon. It will get you used to turn your head to watch the loop. It will build your confidence about handling the rod and learning how to command the ribbon and the line as well. Stay with the ribbon if you like before turning to the fly-line. P.S. The ribbon will not work outside on a windy day.

There is another limitation with the ribbon and rod, but only insofar as your imagination is lacking. You must pretend there is a fly line that comes down from the stripper guide. This is an exercise that will stand you in good stead later when you add a **tugging booster** to your casting. The tugging booster is used predominantly in two situations:

1. When you are **false casting**, which means keeping the line in the air without letting the fly land; and

36

2. When you will be **shooting line**, which means you are adding line to the already amount of line flying. (This is the same tug that was referred to earlier in the generation of kinetic impulse energy.)

In both instances, false casting and shooting line, the tugging booster will make life very much easier for you.

To practice the tugging booster for false casting while you are flying the ribbon, bring your left hand as far up to the stripper guide as it is comfortable for you. Make a backward cast with your left hand positioned up near the stripper guide. When you declare the moment that you should start your forward cast, as you do so, **simultaneously** pretend you are holding the fly line in your left hand and yank down hard until your hand comes down and goes PAST YOUR BUTT. That is a serious tugging booster. Pretend there's a big gong hanging behind you at butt level. Yank the line down from the stripper guide with your fist and with some serious attitude whack that imaginary gong! Your line will behave. It will do what you want it to do. You must match up to your action and move quickly, going back upwards. You are pulling down about a yard (five feet maybe?) of invisible line. As your line goes forward, you must bring your left hand up quickly back to the stripper guide as if the outgoing impulse is pulling the fly line; you pulled down back out on its cast. This works on both the forward and backward cast. For now, just practice it on the forward cast. Then, as your confidence builds, do the tugging booster on both the forward and the backward cast. You'll be surprised how quickly you will move to keep the back and forth synchronized. We'll get to more later but understand the reason now. The tugging booster is like a rocket assist to the impulse energy you must impart to the line. It seriously helps to load the rod.

I must tell you when you get the hang of giving the line the tugging booster when you're false casting, you will fall in love with the action, and you'll false cast longer than you need just because you can do it so well. (Remember on the back cast to send the line straight up from your head!)

The same with shooting line. As you learn to add more and more power to the tugging booster, you will be putting out more and more line than you could even dream of doing when you first started. Watch a long-distance caster, and you will be surprised at how his hand tugging the line works like a piston. As more line goes out, more power is added to the piston—the more straight upward the line is thrown on the backcast.)

The tugging booster, it's a technique that will serve you well in your arsenal.

Come back to re-read this later, but for now, let's continue step by step.

Flying the ribbon, as I suggest, will acclimate you to handling the rod and seeing how it affects the ribbon.

When we replaced the ribbon with the fly line, students amazed themselves on how easy it was to know when the line had straightened out.

They opened the whole world of fly-fishing all by themselves. The mystery of the moment of hesitation was gone. They understood the technique of fly-fishing.

To all my students, I asked only one thing of them. They were to teach what they learned to someone else. This is in keeping with the philosophy of paying forward the fun. We do this by 1. Watching someone fly cast; 2. Learning to fly cast; and 3. Teaching someone to fly cast.

For those students that need some sort of an additional guide to make casts, I came up with a verbal, rhythmical method. I would ask the student to say, "Tick and Tock," stretching out the words to match the flight of the line. As the student watched the line go backward and forward, the student would say "a-a-a-a-a-n-n-n-n-n-n-n-d-d-d-d-d-d. . ." as the loop neared the point where the student anticipated the tug to be, then shouted, "TICK!" at the point he had to tug the line in the opposite direction. The student would watch the loop roll down the line in the opposite direction, and as the loop approached the critical point, again would say, "a-a-a-a-a-n-n-n-n-n-n-n-d-d-d-d-d-d. . ." as the loop neared the point where the student anticipated the tug to be, then shouted, "TOCK!" at the point he had to tug the line in the opposite direction.

This "TICK AND TOCK" gave the students the impression that fly-casting was a rhythmical procedure. Under ideal conditions—with no adjustments necessary—it would be a simple forward and backward exercise. Also, it took the stress out of the exercise. It made it fun, which is precisely what it's all about.

PLATE B. RAINBOW TROUT

5

More on Casting

Here is more information you need to know as you develop into a fly fisherman.

The distance the tip of the rod travels from front to back or from back to front is the amount of energy—swift or slow—applied to the line. This manifests itself in the line by the faster and harder the pull the smaller the loops, the slower and wider the pull the larger the loops. The fisherman will need smaller, harder thrown loops to adjust to a strong wind. The fisherman will want larger loops when there isn't much wind and wants to fish a long line.

Once you have worked with the ribbon, the next step is to go to the rod and line.

Go out on the lawn. Put out about 20 feet of line.

It should be quite easy for you to lay out the line on the lawn in a straight line. Turn around and have it behind you. Capture the fly-line under your hand against the fly rod handle. It will keep the line from going out.

Using the rod, use the point of the rod to go from back to front, pulling the line in front of you and let it land on the lawn. Turn around to put the line behind you and do it again. Here, you're getting a feel of the action of flying a line. If you can do this with confidence, you are well on the road to acquiring the skill.

Next is an exercise just to have you watch the loop in the line unroll down the flying line to its end. When the loop runs out, just let the line land on the lawn. Once again, fly the line before you and just watch the loop unroll to the end of the fly line and then let the line land on the lawn. Do this again as many times as you need to be sure you see the loop travel down the line. You must acknowledge you see this, or you are fooling yourself. This is so critical; you must be positive you see the loop move down the line. If you're not sure, you can't go on to the next exercise. Seeing that loop move down the line is the heart of fly casting.

The next necessary exercise will be fun. Timing the cast involves saying, "TICK AND TOCK." The "TICK" and the "TOCK" are when you pull the rod to fly the line. The "AND" is the extremely critical hesitation part. This is where you stretch out the word while the loop is running out of line. As the loop nears the end of the line, you are saying, "an-an-an-an-an-an-an-anD!" which is your signal to say TOCK and pull the rod in the opposite direction. The trick is to say the "TOCK" at exactly when YOU ANTICIPATE that the loop will reach the end of the line.

Now you must be super-critical of yourself. Did you say "TOCK" at the exact moment the loop ran out of line? Were you a tad early? Were you a bit late? Okay, do it a bit more precisely the next time.

Once you are confident about the TICK-ANNNNNNNNND-TOCK exercise, let's fly the line. We're going to say, 'TICK" using the rod to pull the line that is straight before you on the lawn, which will fly in the air forming a loop that is going behind you, and you will be watching that loop and saying, "Annnnnnn . . ." until you see the loop reach the end of the line when you complete the "And!" and say "TOCK!" to pull the rod before you to energize the line and get the line flying. Now quickly, don't take your eyes off the line flying by you, pick up the loop as you say the drawn-out "And" and watch the loop again until it reaches the end where you say, "TICK" and pull the line in the opposite direction. Watch the loop and do it again.

In making false casts this way, you may have made one or two excellent casts. A couple of them may have caused you distress. That's okay. You're doing it, and you're going to get better and better at making excellent casts.

Let's take a break here to remind you about adjustments. I believe you have become quite aware of it. You will become even more so when you start to consider your reaction time.

The "Annnnnnnd-TOCK" will be the very most critical time. This is the point

That is the most difficult to understand. It is the point that causes the most trouble. It is the least understood of all the principles of fly casting. It is the hardest to explain and to teach for the very reasons I have already said about making an adjustment to a variety of conditions and situations as well as going so far back in the elementary lessons.

At this point, as a student, I would suggest you play role reversal with yourself.

Pretend you are the teacher, and you are trying to teach a novice what fly casting is all about. If your explanations do not make sense, stop what you're doing and go back to the beginning. It will save you a lot of time. There is no winner in the card game solitaire. Only you are the winner when you can fly-cast.

The next step is to adjust and correct your timing.

Here you must learn at what point you must move the rod to start another cast.

The point, of course, is where in the line is the ending loop when you command yourself to energize the rod to fly the line in the opposite direction. For some, the loop may be a yard from the end of the line, for others a foot from the end. Trial and error will do it for you. Don't be impatient. You may learn how to tie wind-knots before you make that perfect cast, but you will do make that one perfect cast, which will lead you to a lifetime of others.

The recommendation is that you start with a short length of line rather than a longer one. Gradually you can add line as your confidence increases.

By starting out casting shorter lengths of line, one can watch the loop and ANTICIPATE when it will straighten out. The line will tell you what you are doing. If you apply the pull too early, you will snap the end or make a "crack" sound. If you apply the energy too late, the line will go into a wind knot or bird's nest or fall and hit the ground.

The pull to start the next cast must be smooth, not choppy, as using a bullwhip. We can do this and get the timing right if we think of a metronome. A metronome is used primarily by music teachers to instruct pupils on the exact timing needed to perform music. Timing must be exact when performing with other musicians to make sure everyone is in the same place in the music. If not, imagine the cacophony.

Thus, casting a fly line can be put to the steady beat of a metronome—tick and tock, tick and tock, tick and tock. Here the "and" between the tick/tock is the reaction time allowance. This is the well-known "hesitation" we hear about in fly-casting.

The "Tick" is the initial pull of the line that forms the loop that travels down the line.

The "And" is the hesitation while waiting for the line to straighten out.

The "Tock" is the re-energization of the line in the opposite direction.

Here is how I would time my casts: I would say, "Tick!" to start the cast going from front to back. Then, I would say, "A-n-n-n-n-n-n-n-n . . ." as I waited for the crucial point where I know my reaction time begins, and say,

". . . n-n-d!" and say, "Tock!" to start my forward cast. So, it would sound like: "Tick Annnnnnnnnnnd Tock! Then, again, "Tick Annnnnnnnnnnd Tock!" as we're flying the line back and forth. Remember, the back and forth comes very quickly, so be prepared.

The timing will change as we lengthen or shorten the amount of line we're flying.

The timing will change if we put more energy into the rod, which will make smaller loops.

The timing will change if we put less energy into the rod, which will make larger loops.

The timing will change if the wind comes up or changes direction.

The timing will change if you're just having that kind of a day.

The timing is just part of the adjustments we continually must make fly-fishing.

To cut down on your practice time to learn when to anticipate the time to re-energize the line, I have come up with a very visual method that slows down the action of the fly-cast and makes you familiar with a method of more accurately anticipating when to pull the rod forward or backward.

Another way to anticipate when to pull the rod is by feeling when the loop is ending. Let's wait before we get into this.

Remember, the art in fly casting is adjusting. This would be a good place to point out your reaction time will have to be adjusted as you start casting longer and longer lengths of line. Once you know what to look for, the rest comes easily. A longer length of line naturally will have a longer waiting time for the loop to straighten out.

We'll get to a method I will show you that will make everything very visual to you. We'll exchange explanation with visualization.

Coming up, I will provide you with a technique for making this point quite visible.

The second way to know when the line is straightened out is by feel. It is subtle, and it must be discerned, and with care, the shifting action will be noted. With careful attention, the feel becomes second nature, and so will the adjustment for reaction time.

The gold medal of fly casting is when you no longer must watch the fly line to know when to change direction. A simple answer would be that you develop a "feel" for what is happening with the line. The best explanation is that it is a trained, educated response. Suddenly the timing becomes second nature because you've performed the action so many times. You will find you are not watching the loop but concentrating on something else. Say, where you want to land the fly. You just KNOW when it's time to tug the line in the opposite direction. This will happen when you least expect it. Suddenly, you blink your eyes rapidly, and you'll say to yourself, "Holy Martoley! I could just feel when it was the right time to fly the line in the other direction." Usually, it happens when you're distracted, and you just do what you've practiced. That, Sir/Madam, is when you have arrived.

6

Line Control

Here's a method to **visually** reveal the mystery of the fly-cast. The mystery centers on **control of the line**. The mystery has to do with the hesitation while waiting for all the energy to dissipate from a cast before applying new energy to make it go in the opposite direction. It will show very clearly your reaction time! That hesitation is the make or break of fly casting. Here's a method to make you see the actual point where your reaction time comes into play and how long the hesitation should be in the action of casting a fly line. Here are the essential elements.

You will need a ribbon about a half-inch wide, and about 10-12 feet long. Ordinary ribbon or tape will do.

Attach the ribbon to the top guide of your bare fly rod.

Hold the rod and allow the ribbon to dangle before you.

Turn the end of the rod in circles. Notice the ribbon follows the tip of the rod precisely. You are the director, and the ribbon obeys your every movement. Without fail, the ribbon will trace small or large circles, quickly or slowly, as you command. Make the circles just with your wrist, then with your forearm, and then with your entire arm. The ribbon is a slave to your wishes.

Does this feel like child's play? It is because it's that simple, and it's that simple to cast a fly.

Your thoughts are to experiment with other figures. Go to it. Make circles over your head, straight-line movements, or you can write your name.

It has come to my attention that women acquire the skill of fly-casting much faster and easier than men. The reason I was given was women make better use of the rod and line. Men want to use their arm strength to drive the mechanics. They must un-learn the stiff arm, such as is used in wielding the tennis racquet, or the sidearm flapping elbow that baseball pitchers use. Unless you have someone watching you who can point these out to you, the caution would be to relax, take it—not easy—but easier.

As long as you continue to move the rod, you energize—which is a key-word—the ribbon, and it is that energy that keeps it in the air or flying. When you keep the ribbon—or fly line—in the air flying back and forth, front to back, this is called **false casting.** A real cast is when the angler allows the fly line to land.

The instant you stop moving the rod, the ribbon is no longer **energized**. It will begin to collapse and will continue to collapse until it is either re-energized or flops loosely at the end of the rod or whatever you're using. This is an essential lesson in fly line control. Broadly, the degree of movement used to energize the fly rod is equal to the energy imparted to the fly line. When the fly rod is stopped, the fly line will continue to fly until it dissipates the energy that was imparted to it. Another example would be throwing a baseball straight up into the air. It will continue to go upwards until the energy applied to it is gone or used up, then it begins its descent. The more energy applied to the baseball, the higher it goes, and so on. It is the same with the fly line, flying until its energy is gone, and then it gradually collapses.

Controlling the amount of energy and the length of time the energy is applied to the fly rod also controls the rate at which the line collapses and is the key to making the proper presentation of an artificial fly.

Simply, a proper presentation of a fly on the water is made by a **controlled collapse** of the fly line. This is what fly-fishing is all about. This is done by under-standing the dynamics of the rod and line, which is pretty much what you have done with the rod and tape. When you pull the tape backward notice, the tape forms a loop. To have a ten-foot piece of ribbon fly back and forth at the end of a rod, it merely needs a continuous back and forth movement. With the short distance, the ribbon is re-energized by the pull in the opposite direction before it begins to collapse. Because of the air resistance, it is difficult to make a very long piece of ribbon fly, but if one were able to do that, one noticeable difference would become apparent between the varying lengths. It takes a longer time for the energy to dissipate and reach the end of the longer ribbon than it does a shorter piece. That means the angler must hesitate or wait until the end of the ribbon has become straight, and its energy dissipated before he can impart energy to move it in the opposite direction. Notice the rule stated earlier. It is this momentary hesitation that causes the most significant difficulty in learning to cast a fly. It is the "and" in tick and tock exercise. The answer to overcoming this difficulty is to watch the fly line until you get the "feel" of the fly cast. As the arc in the line moves toward the end, say "tick" and while waiting for it to reach the end say,

46

"and," then when the loop nears the point where it will straighten out, say "tock" and at that point re-energize the line.

This is the point to notice that if you pull the line forward before the loop has reached the end of the line, it is because you have a very quick reaction time that re-energizes the line prematurely. In this case, you must wait that extra fraction of a second before you re-energize the line. The opposite is also true. If your reaction time is slow, and you fail to re-energize the line before the loop reaches the end, the line will run out of energy and will collapse. For this, either adjust your reaction time to be faster or start re-energizing the line a bit sooner.

Now, if energy is imparted before it is fully opened, that is, the arc has not reached the end of the line, what would happen? The answer is that the end is being yanked around to try to catch up to itself. It doing so, it must **break the sound barrier or go faster than the speed of sound**. Doing that, it would break the speed of sound. The end of the ribbon snaps out loud. Anglers lose their flies when they do this, so snapping off a fly should be avoided. As you begin using the rod and fly line, you may find you are tying knots in the end of the line. These are called "wind knots" even though the wind has nothing to do with them. The uneven action—such as when you want to snap a stock whip—is the cause of wind knots.

Here's how to snap the ribbon, so you will know what not to do when you are fly-casting.

Fly the ribbon front to back in a nice steady and slow rhythm. Watch the ribbon as it straightens out. As the ribbon is flying backward and just before the loop has straightened out, abruptly snap your wrist forward. The two energies clash and cause a problem. It should make a loud report. If it does not, then vary the time you are snapping your wrist until the ribbon breaks the speed of sound, forms a vacuum, the air rushing in to fill the void creates the aftershock. You will notice the faster you snap the ribbon back on itself, the louder the sound. Practice this until you can do it three times in a row (in using the stock whip, this action is called "cutting the snake"). The stock whip makes the sound of a pistol shot and is used to control cattle. By then, you will have the technique and the understanding of how it happens. In technical terms, you have caused the end of the ribbon to exceed the velocity of the speed of sound, which is approximately 1,100 feet per second! Air rushing in to fill the void created the sound just as it does after lightning strikes, and we hear thunder, the sonic boom of a jet going through the sound barrier, or the Crack! of a stock whip in action.

The end of the line is trying to catch up to the speeding line before it and needs to break the sound barrier to do it.

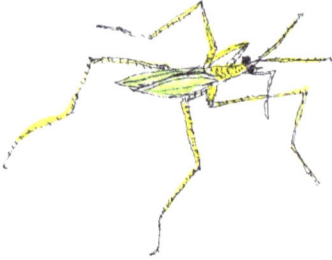

28. WATER STRIDER

29. BLACKFLY – LARVA, ADULT

30. ANT

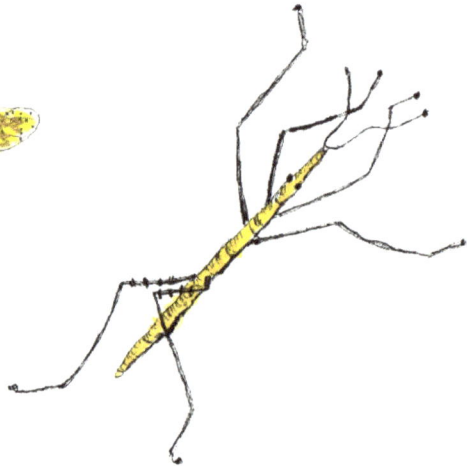

31. BEE

32. WALKING STICK

7

Leverage

You were able to do this because of **leverage**. Leverage is the product of the distance traveled and time. The formula for leverage is V=dt, or velocity equals distance times time. Leverage is acquired when we exchange energy at the hand for speed at the tip of the rod. The energy at the hand is applied over only a few inches, whereas the speed at the tip of the rod covers at least a foot. Nature keeps things in balance by exchanging one for the other: the power at the hand for dissipation of the energy over a longer arc at the end of the rod. Leverage is what enables a hammer to drive in a spike. Consider now that when you are fly-casting, you may be using a nine-foot fly-casting rod! Imagine the exchange of power for speed in this situation.

To go back to the ribbon, there is one more aspect to practice. Hold the rod in your hand and raise your arm directly over your head as if one were the extension of the other. Use your entire arm to make the ribbon form circles. Now, bring the arm down, holding the elbow tight to your body, and using just the elbow make the ribbon form circles. Next, with your elbow still at your side, use just your wrist to make the ribbon form circles. It will be evident the circles made with the full-arm were somewhat slower, covered a greater distance, and took more energy. The use of the elbow as a pivot point created faster circles, covered less of a distance, and took less energy. Finally, the wrist created the fastest circles, covered even less of a distance, and took less energy. The reason for this, as you know, is because of leverage. Small action at the wrist, big action at the rod tip.

Each of these techniques will be used in fly-casting, but the use or non-use of the wrist must be emphasized as the most important. This has to do with leverage and technique. Anchor your elbow in at your side. Hold the rod straight up.

Just bending your wrist move the tip of the rod from the twelve on the clock face toward the eleven. You may just about be able to make it that far. (Bending the wrist this far backward while casting is blamed for tailing knots, ground hits, lost control. See Introduction.) On the backstroke, the tip of the rod might be able to reach the numeral two. That is the limit of the arc you can strike when you break (bend) the wrist. This seems like a short distance but consider the leverage and the short arc made by the wrist and the length of the arc at the tip. The wrist alone is not enough to generate the power needed for longer casts, however. The wrist break is added seamlessly to the forearms' rhythmic back and forth. If you do not focus too much on the cast at this point, as your forearm moves back and forth with the elbow held tight to the body, the wrist will automatically go into a break, accelerating the tip of the rod. To visualize this vital wrist action, go back to the ribbon. Visualize a symphony conductor moving the rod as you are casting frontwards and backward. Smoothly does it. The acceleration comes on like a painted line. Women get this very easily. They let the dynamics of the cast work for them. Men rely on muscle power, which gets them into trouble. We do not want the wrist snap used to make the stock whip "Cra-ack!" Just the opposite. Think of just pointing back and forth from the 11 to the 2 to accelerate the tip of the rod. Add this to the motion of the forearm as it moves forward, and you will have the casting action. To accelerate the tip on the backward cast, the forward bent wrist is snapped backward but is jerked to a stop when it is in a straight line with the arm. This provides forceful, dynamic action to the rod and the line. Bending the wrist back further than straight in-line diminishes the action because, in effect, when the tip of the rod is pointing past the number two to the three or four on the clock face, it is trying to change the flight of the line from upward to downward. The wrist over-bend is blamed for the tailings, and so on. The wrist strap was designed to prevent this (or tuck the end of the rod in the shirt sleeve). Should you have a problem, go back to the ribbon, and watch your wrist waggle. In a few casts, you will see where you need to stop the further bending action of the wrist and note it is straight in line with your arm.

The action of the wrist is important because it provides leverage to the rod, which essentially is a lever. Think of the rod as being connected to a pin just below the reel, which allows the rod to move back and forth. In physics, this would be called the fulcrum. The load on which this lever acts is the tip of the fly rod (to which is connected the fly-line). The power or force to move the load is the fly caster's hand, which is between the reel and the tip. Examples of this type of lever are the broom and the baseball bat. The hand at the top of the broom is the fulcrum. The other hand, about a third way down the broom handle, provides the power. The load is the broomcorn that does the sweeping. In fly-fishing, the short arc at the wrist is magnified by a much larger arc at the tip of the rod. This provides the leverage required to make a cast.

The essential action in the casting force is to pretend that instead of a fly-rod, you are holding a double-headed hammer. On the clock face, instead of the numbers ten and two replace them with jutting out at right angles either tacks, large two-penny nails, or spikes, or any variety of nail in between. The force on your forward or backward strokes would be like driving, in say, the nail. For example, on a very windy day, your action would be to strike in the spikes forcefully. Whereas, if you were close in on a small stream and you had to finesse the line and fly to a spot a short distance away, your action would be to tap in the tacks.

Once again, watch an experienced fly-caster. Their action may be character-ized as "gentle fluidity." If you understand this, you may not get it on your early casts, but with patience, you will acquire the vital proper wrist/arm technique.

On another matter, you may not have noticed as you were running the tape back and forth that you were instinctively making an oval with the tip of the rod. If you didn't, the rod and the tape would collide because they were on the same line of travel, or a road in the same lane. You gave the rod and the tape room to pass one another. The different planes are not as important now as they will be when you are fly-casting.

33. CRICKET

34. SKIMMER

35. ROYAL COACHMAN

36. COACHMAN

37. GILT COACHMAN

38. ORANGE COACHMAN

39. PALE EVENING DUN

8

Rule No. 1

By this time, you are confident about flying the ribbon in any direction on any plane: back and forth, over your shoulders, between your legs, around your ankles, behind your neck, writing your sweetheart's name. All of this will make you a versatile fly caster. Even though you may not have expressed it out loud, you are very much aware now, especially of the first rule of fly-fishing.

RULE NO. ONE:

AS THE TIP GOES, SO FOLLOWS THE LINE.

There are times that the end of the fly line, leader, tippet, and fly do not collapse gently but crash and splash onto the surface. Generally, this happens when the line is over-powered. Instead of allowing the loop to carry the line further, which the contained energy will allow it to do, the fisherman causes the line to crash-land. Too much power, too short a cast. Should you see that is going to happen, the only hope of rescue is to drop the entire rod parallel to and almost touching the water. But the action is so fast; the water is splashing before you realize what's happened. The best answer is to collect yourself. Start over, and fish that same spot five or ten minutes later (that's the big guy's honey spot, and he's not a-going to let another fish have it).

Before moving on to the rod and line, feel very comfortable and confident with the rod and tape. You may want to use a longer tape and overcome any difficulties you may encounter in making small or large curls, or in snapping the tape. Then, working the rod and line will be more fine-tuning rather than frustration. Should you run into a problem with the rod and line, go back to the tape to identify the cause and resolve the difficulty, especially if you don't have someone to check you out. The right kind of practice will make you a master caster.

The next step up the skill ladder is becoming familiar with your fly rod. It is surprising how quickly you move up these steps because you are using your progress to guide you. With that comes confidence in yourself. First, you can tell exactly how well you are doing. Second, because you want to do this, you want to do it as best as you are able. And, third, you are keeping track of yourself and have no one else to impress. You may wish to keep going back over and over some aspect until you get it exactly right. You're getting it almost perfect for yourself, not for anyone else. Use the mantra of the European craftsman, "Make-a nice!"

You will need a piece of ribbon about a foot longer than your fly rod tied to the tip-top guide.

With the guides facing downwards, grip the handle of the rod with your thumb extended on top, pointing to the tip. This is the more practical style because the thumb adds power to the rod on the forward cast, and when you become proficient casting a fly, your thumb will be used to point to the spot you want the fly to land. The thumb off to one side of the handle allows the rod to bend backward further for more power, say. Combine an off-thumb backward bend with a wrist bend, and I guarantee trouble unless there is a specific reason for dropping the tip so low. There may be times when you may have reason to do this. For example, to gain leverage on the backward angle for throwing a more powerful impulse into the line.

We stay with the ribbon for this exercise because it provides a slow-motion semblance of the action of a fly-line. We will come back to the ribbon further on. We say "semblance" because the weight of the fly-line is necessary to properly load the fly rod for casting, which the ribbon is unable to do. So, within this limitation, put the ribbon through a variety of movements as you did earlier with the rod.

Concentrate now on the action of the fly rod when you are fly-casting. Practice striking an arc.

Picture your shoulder against the center of a large clock face. With the rod held straight up, it will be before the numeral 12. The clock face has been used since antiquity to have the fly-fisherman gauge his backward and forward rod movements. It still works. Disregard the clock face if you will. It must work for you.

Because we must cast the line backward as well as forward to energize the rod, we limit the swing of the rod between the numerals ten on the forward cast and two on the backward cast. This action will keep the line in the air or "flying."

As you practice, you will become aware that three elements affect the two-to-ten arc. They are the amount of energy applied to the rod, the speed of the rod back and forth, and the suppleness or stiffness of the rod. Because of these elements, you may stop the movement of your rod at the two, or the ten, but the tip of the rod because of the supple spring action will continue past these numbers. With experience, you will adjust any or all of these elements to keep the arc of the rod between the two and the ten to make the line fly properly, or between nine and three o'clock, if you wish. You will notice as the rod reaches the end of its arc, it speeds up because of (wrist) leverage and momentum.

Pivoting from your elbow, keep the arm and rod as one solid unit and use the wrist to make the ribbon fly as you swing forward and backward with the rod moving between the ten and the two. With this, you will understand the importance of the wrist to provide the subtle needed action to the rod and line.

This is an easy and safe way to get the hang of fly-casting.

You must watch the action of the ribbon as you vary the speed of your casts.

You will notice **the loop** at the end of the ribbon will be tighter or wider depending on how wide and how fast you swing the rod. When you start using the fly-line, you will know that narrow loops are more desirable then wide-open loops. The wider the swing of the rod, the wider the loops.

Should you slow down a good bit, you will notice it requires a little longer hesitation before you re-energize the ribbon by moving in the opposite direction. You must identify this action, so stay with it until you can identify it accurately. If you are not sure, speed up your casts until you start snapping the ribbon then ease back into slow motion.

To emphasize how important this is, you should be aware that at one time, someone invented a contraption that locked the arm to the body and forced the would-be angler's rod arm to move in an erratic, awkward, jerking motion.

To understand energizing a line, you can see it also when you snap a rope.

Another teaching method was to strap a cigar box between the elbow and the body to make sure the elbow was used as the pivot point.

Remember to experiment with the rod and ribbon in every way possible just for the fun of it. Spend a little extra time on this because it puts you in touch with rod control. Later, with the fly line, as your technique progresses, you will find it easy to learn how to make the fly "turn a corner" with a sideways motion rather than with a back and forth motion. It will enable you to drop a fly behind a rock or a protruding log or bush. The skilled fly casters who know how to do this say it is "making a right-angle turn." This serves to emphasize the rule that as the tip goes, so goes the line. As usual, practice now will pay off later.

One exercise that calls for the technique to master the skill is what is called "mending" the line. Mend, in this case, means to alter the flight of the line. A fly-fisherman would mend the line if he didn't want the current to pull at the line causing the fly to run unnaturally, which would caution the fish. In mending the line, just before the fly lands, the fisherman would cause the tip of the rod to scribe an arc, like scribing a line that "crosses like an arc over a bridge." This simply means to strike a horizontal arc either to the left or the right to make the line curve in an upstream direction. This adjustment causes the line to ride downstream with the current to prevent an awkward, unnatural movement of the fly. Without the mend, the current against the line would immediately pull the fly downstream in an unusual manner that would caution a fish. The reason the line with a loop working can be altered by the mend is that the impulse action is not contrary to the original impulse action put into the loop but is moving the line sideways.

Let's put the fly rod and the fly line together.

The reel is seated at the end of the rod behind the handle. Put the reel in place and fasten it securely by turning the threaded ring up to hold it. Some fly-casters prefer to keep the reel in their vest pockets. The reasons include keeping the rod lightweight, personal preference, and finding the reel superfluous in fly-fishing. The line should come out of the reel through the wide hole, which should face the top of the rod.

Thread the fly line through the guides, missing none.

Tie a leader to the end of the fly line and tie a tippet onto the leader but do not tie on a fly but rather a little piece of wool. The wool hitting the back of your head by accident will not hurt as much as getting stuck with a hook. Also, the wool, for the most part, will keep down the sound barrier noise.

9

Fly the line

Let out the line about two times the length of your fly rod. Using the ten-to-two arc, **fly the line.** That is, let the line fly back and forth. Although advanced fly-casting involves two hands—one on the rod and the other guiding the line—all you need do at this time is hold the line under your hand at the handle. Get the feel of the line in the air watching it all the while. You will notice the difference between the line and the ribbon. The line flies easier because it's meant to do so. The technique remains the same: watch the line as it flies, forms loops, is re-energized, and flies in the opposite direction. Be sure to watch the line as it goes back and forth, and you'll soon get the picture of what is to come with long, graceful casts. Do not be concerned at this time about being distracted because you need to watch the line. Your only focus at this point is to master the line.

Ideally, the fly line should run back and forth on the same plane. Because of many factors, it cannot do the ideal, so the next best thing to do is to tilt the plane, so it is lower in the front and higher in the back. The reverse is not at all desired because it makes line control more difficult.

Keeping the line in the air in this fashion is used for three purposes while fly-fishing:

1. To let out or take in line.

2. To dry off a fly; and

3. To pause or re-direct the line to a landing spot.

The next step is to make **the cast**. This is the controlled collapse.

If you stop the movement of the rod, as you know, the line will collapse on its own. You need to control the collapse because you want accuracy to put the fly in a spot on the water. If you stop the action of the rod, willy-nilly, the line may end up behind you or at your feet.

To get control, stop moving the rod when your thumb on the rod generally points to the spot you want the cast to go. That's it!

Fly the line, pick a spot, point your thumb, and stop the rod.

If you're doing this on a lawn and you have about fifteen feet of line out, you'll find you can lay the line down pretty close to your target. This is an exercise, so you may want to do this a dozen times or so picking different targets. Remember to watch the line as it flies because you need a smooth cast. Be patient with yourself and don't settle for a poor cast. Use the rod as the center post on a metronome used by piano teachers to have their students keep precise time. Your back and forth and back and forth should be the same, keeping an even, steady beat. Break that beat, and you either snap the line or tie a wind knot. Keep adjusting until you are confident you have the cast under control. Payback will come later.

Very quickly, you might believe you can put out even a longer length of line, but before you do that, get to do the next step correctly right from the beginning. It is the technique of getting a line airborne when it's lying at rest. There is an advanced technique for doing this that takes a giant tug, which requires the use of both hands. For now, keep the short length of line held in place by your rod hand.

10

Backcast Technique

Question: Where does the fly line go on the backcast?

To answer this question, even experienced anglers will turn around and point directly behind them. Using the clock face, they may turn from number nine and point to number three. That may be true, but that is not the way the angler should *think,* and not the way I taught fly casting.

The idea is to over-compensate on the backcast. I would tell my students the backcast may go behind them, but they must think of casting the line directly overhead for the backcast! They must think of whipping the tip of the rod straight up in line with twelve o'clock! Yes, put a target in the sky directly overhead and attempt to have the tip of the fly-line hit that target. My rule was to point directly overhead. I would say, "You are not to cast behind you, but cast directly over your head!" To do that, I suggest they have the back of their rod hand parallel with the sky and to try to hit the sky with the back of the hand. It looks like an awkward cast, but it does the job. That's where you should *think* the backcast must go. Of course, the line cannot go directly overhead, but it forces the fly-caster to "think" of casting and making the motion with the rod of casting straight up. I know you have read and understood this, but I am going to explain my thinking about the backcast again, and then repeat it later. It's that important. You won't appreciate the technique now. You will on the stream.

Again, on the backcast: Should you be told you're bending your wrist too much and told you should be wearing a wrist band, follow these instructions. If you pluck the frog correctly, you won't need it. The reason is when you pluck the frog and making the backcast that's supposed to go straight over your head, then

40. BLACK GNAT

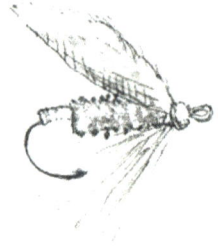

42. WHITE MILLER

41. SCARLET IBIS

43. PARKER

45. DUN WING

44. PARMACHEENE BELLE

48. CLARET SPINNER

46. DUSTY MILLER

47. RED ATTRACTOR

the action of your hand on the rod should be as if it moves up in a straight line from your belt to just above your head. (NOT backward to the two o'clock position on the clock.) Keep the back of your rod hand facing the sky and put some speedy energy into raising your hand as straight upward as you're able. Think of drawing a straight line with the back of your hand from the tips of your shoes, past your nose, and straight-up! That's the action of getting a high backward cast to create a high plane behind you. When you do that, you just can't bring the tip of the rod behind you lower than the two on the clock face. You won't be over-bending your wrist, and you won't need a wrist strap!

The reason for doing this is that it emphasizes that the line should go as high as possible on the backcast. This is very much desired and achieves a "tilted plate" plane of the casts, which is coming up.

Allow me to repeat this in different words. On the backcast, the angler should fool himself. He knows the line must go behind him, but if he thinks that way, the line will drop too low and may even hit the ground (especially if he's not wearing a wrist strap and allows his wrist to bend way too much. I apologize for the sarcasm.) So, to counter this, the angler must think that the line must be thrown directly, straight above the head. Yes, on the backcast, the angler must believe the line must extend from the tip of his nose and go up in a straight line. The line won't do that, of course, but it will keep the back-cast high. The action of the hand will move straight upwards, which will keep the back-cast high. I cannot over-emphasize this enough.

This would be an excellent place to bring up the plane of the forward and backward casts. First, make an underlined note that the forward and backward casts are mirror images of one another. But exactly. Or they should be. Yet, I speak about keeping the back-cast high. This refers to the plane of the casts. Think of the plane as a flat dish sitting atop your head, then tilt the back of the dish upwards by about a 15-degree angle. A straight-line drawn front to back is the plane you should be working as you make your false casts—high in the back, lower in the front, but mirror images of one another. Does the concept still elude you? Draw a stick figure. Draw a line touching the top of the head perpendicular to the body. Now, angle that line so it goes upwards in the back and down by the same amount in front. That's the plane to shoot for, although you should make adjustments to suit yourself.

To pick up a line lying on the lawn requires a "sharp stroking action," or as I say, a big, snappy tug. We get into the wrist again. It would be great if your wrists were as strong as a by-hand cow milker but use whatever you've got to get the leverage you need to overcome the inertia of a line at rest. We need this to overcome the law of physics that says, "A body at rest tends to stay at rest." On the clock face, the tip of the rod would be jerked up sharply from eight o'clock, and it would stop abruptly at eleven o'clock. That's when the tip of the rod is pointing straight above your head. The abruptness will supply the extra-needed power to get the fly line airborne. Here's an image you may visualize to remember: Pluck an imaginary frog off the top of the water with the tip of your pole and send it flying straight high into the air! To repeat, the line will not go directly over your head, of course, but if you think that way, it will send the line behind you in a high altitude. This is the time to let the line know what you've got. Grunt if you must like the pro tennis players, but power that line! Also, the extra energy generated will be needed to break the cohesive force of the water, holding down the fly line.

A high line altitude is very desirable. It helps you **fight against gravity,** which tends to pull the line lower to the ground or water. Should you not give enough power on the pickup or backward cast, and not aim high over your head, it may descend and touch down behind you. You will know when that happens, remember, because you've been watching the line. That's a bad cast. When it happens, stop, regroup, and start over.

This wasn't mentioned before to get you quickly to this point, but when just flying the line, the attitude of the fly-caster should be on the backward cast to send the line as high into the air as possible. Thinking "high, straight over the head," will get the fly-caster the control that is needed to make those long, graceful, accurate casts. With just a line and no hook, practice the motion of tossing the line directly over your head. Pluck that frog off the water and toss it to that point right over your head! This action will be so important when you have become confident with casting the fly, and you start shooting for longer and longer distances. The need to think of backcasting the line directly over your head is mandatory for distance casting.

Essentially, what this technique does is make you think that everything is in slow motion and allows you plenty of time to allow your hand, eye, mind coordination. I say it eases up the grunt work.

11

Rod Dynamics

Moving up to the next step in fly casting, we come to what is called "**loading the rod.**" A more understanding way is to say, "put a bend in the rod!" An easy way to understand this is to consider how a slingshot works. A patch to hold the missile is connected to rubber bands that are attached to separate arms of a "Y." To fire the missile, the patch is pulled back, stretching the rubber bands. Releasing the patch sends the missile on its way.

Instead of rubber bands, the fly-fishing rod uses its suppleness to be loaded—bent—with the propelling power, just like the rubber bands. If one could anchor the handle of a fly rod and load a missile in the eye of the top eyelet then bend back the tip of the rod as far as it can go without breaking it then releasing it, the missile will fly off, the same as missiles were propelled by a catapult. That is precisely how the fly road works when the line bends it back to load it with energy. The natural action of the loaded fly rod will fling the line forward with no further effort on the part of the fisherman. Of course, the distance will not be far, but shoot forward it will.

To load the rod essentially means to supply or fill the rod with energy that it will use to aid in casting a line. It is the same as pulling back a drawstring on a bow to have it fly an arrow. Here the drawstring loads or puts energy into the bow. In fly-fishing, the line loads the rod. The released energy is the same except with a bow one looses an arrow, and with a fly rod, one creates impulse energy to propel a fly line. The fly rod is loaded both on the forward and on the backward cast. On the forward cast, the entire rod, but mainly the tip, is bent rearward by the line and the energy put into it. As the action or spring in the rod is released, its energy is used to send the line forward. On the back cast, the action is the reverse as the forward bend releases its energy to send the line behind the caster. The less the rod is loaded, the shorter the cast. The more energy put into the rod to load it, the longer the cast.

The rod is loaded when the rod is started on a forward or backward cast, then stopped at either the ten or two o'clock position. The energy put into the line causes the rod to bend, thus loading the rod with energy.

I'm afraid you may have anticipated the next instruction. You may have already used it on your own to overcome the inertia of a line on the ground to get it into the air. We're talking about the tugging booster we described much earlier with the "invisible" line.

The supplementary way to assist in loading the rod is the tugging booster. It requires the "free" hand to add a short, sharp tug booster to the line downwards as the cast is started. That same snap of the line aids in breaking water tension when picking up line that is lying on the surface of the water, when working the line against the wind, or when setting the hook. Without the tug by the second hand, the resistance of the line—flying or at rest—would allow the topmost guide to slide back down the line until the rod has been loaded—bent—to the point where its resistance is greater and works to pull the line. What also helps here is the thought to send the line straight above your head.

12

Shooting the line

The importance of loading the rod is to enable the angler to **shoot line**. "Shooting the line" is not an execution. It is a method of "putting out more line" or "making the line longer" or "adding more line to be flown." It is the action of adding to the line to make it longer while it is flying.

Line may be added on the forward or the backward cast.

To add line, line must be available—in reserve, if you will—in loose coils ready to fly freely through the rod's guides. There is too much resistance pulling the line wound on the reel. Trying to shoot line by having it unwind from the reel isn't worth another word. Don't waste your time. Thus, the line must first be stripped free from the reel and held in loose coils. It is done so the line will be free to run loose when the fisherman "shoots" the line. To avoid tangles, there is a little box made that sits on the fly fisherman's chest into which the line is collected as it is pulled in. Shooting line is a complicated procedure, much like patting your head and rubbing your belly. Don't try to master shooting line too soon, or you may become discouraged. If your fly-casting technique up to this point is built on a firm foundation, shooting line will come quickly if you understand what is going on with your technique and adjusting.

Shooting line is the action of the impulse energy in the flying line pulling out more line with it. Shooting line requires a two-handed technique, one hand on the handle controlling the rod's action, and the other hand guiding the out or in of the line through the ferrules. The difference between the short snap described earlier to break water cohesion is that the downward tug is made for a greater distance and that the line can run out freely for a distance before it is stopped.

While looking at a fly-fisherman shooting line, it looks as if he is stretching out a thick rubber band held between his hands and then closing them. The hand on the rod is pulling it up and away, and the other hand is pulling down and away going behind his butt. When the fisherman shoots the line, the lower hand shoots straight up, past the other hand, and—with the line slipping loosely through it—right up to the stripper guide. That's where the line will be stopped and trapped and yanked back down again.

Shooting line is a three-part procedure:

- Yanking the line downwards to load the rod to start either the backward or frontwards cast (the topmost guide slides down the line, remember).
- Releasing the hold on the line just as the impulse energy of the out-going cast line pulls out a length of spare line along with it; and
- Grabbing again and holding the line behind the stripper guide before too much line goes out (which, if too burdensome, would exhaust the impulse energy causing the line to collapse, and this is used to cast a fly).

Shooting line requires critical timing—twice. The first time is when the fisherman releases his hold on the line allowing the momentum of the flying line to form a loop that has the impulse and energy to pull more line out. The second critical timing is when the fisherman must grab the line to stop any more line from flying out, keeping the impulse energy working rather than killing it with an overload of line. If the line isn't stopped and the line continues to slip through the guides, its drag will supersede and overcome the impulse and cause the line to collapse.

The hand with the line must either allow the line to slip through it, or to hold it tightly. When the line is held firmly, it allows the angler to fly the line forward and backward without letting out or taking in line. If the line were not held firmly, the line would merely slip through the guides, unable to load the rod. The action of shooting line is that the line is held tightly while the rod is being loaded. The line is then released as the rod unloads, and just before the rod straightens out from the unloading, the line must be released by sort of pushing it up and out through the stripper guide and guides. It is a timed pull-and-release rhythm that allows the line to take the loose line through the holding hand. There is a small window—depending on how fast the line is going out—for the line shooting because the line itself must be grabbed very quickly in time to cause the rod to re-load. The angler then holds it firmly again as the line reaches the

PLATE C. LARGE-MOUTH BLACK BASS

end of its impulse, so the angler may once again load the rod. It is pretty much a shoot-the-line then stop any more line from going out.

At what point in the cast does one know when to shoot the line?

This is a matter of timing to know when to release your hold on the line. This is a simple matter of flying the line with the line hand up by the stripper guide and swinging them in unison back and forth as the fisherman flies the line. The method to learn when to release the line is to concentrate on the hand holding the line. As the rod goes back and forth, the hand holding the line works in a pumping action up to the stripper guide, then down past the reel at the end of the fly-rod, then up again to the stripper guide, and so on.

There are two techniques for shooting the line.

The first technique is to get more line flying to have the fly reach a greater distance. This means the fisherman will continue to shoot line on each forward and backward cast until he is flying as much line as he thinks he needs. As line is added, the fisherman must adjust for the increased need for impulse power required to fly the line making false casts. The more line out, the more power needed to fly the line. That is a given whether one is shooting line or making false casts.

The second technique is to shoot the line—usually on the forward cast—and allow the fly to land. A fisherman will do this if he is fishing the waters incrementally from his position and is reaching out a little further on each cast.

Tug and Cast

False casting will be quite easy once you can shoot line. Once you have the technique of tugging the line downwards, you will marvel at your skill to false cast backward and forward as many times as you have the endurance to perform. (Remember reading earlier the invisible line with the rod and tape?) What action you retain from shooting the line is the downwards tug of the line. The big difference is you do not release the line at any time. As you lift the rod to fly the line, reach up to the stripper guide, grab the fly line firmly, and with enthusiasm, tug the line down with a straight arm until it goes past your body at butt level. As the impulse energy pulls at the line as it usually would if you were shooting line, hold tightly to the line and allow the line to pull your hand up to the stripper guide where it will be ready to yank the line down again for the reverse cast. Over-emphasize this up and down sawing motion with your hand holding the line. Soon you will be false casting to beat the band. Do not forget your technique of thinking to cast the line directly over your head on the backward cast. The action will amaze you as you get into the rhythm of tug and cast, tug and cast. The caution is to not over-power the cast on a short line, which is easy to do.

As you get better and better at it, now and then shoot out a little more line and keep your line hand pumping.

Along with casting the line out, there is a technique for bringing the line in. To **retrieve the line** quickly, the line is run over the index finger of the hand holding the rod and pulled in and collected in large loops with the other hand. Care must be taken not to have the collected line end up in a massive snarl. To counter this line is collected in chest or hip buckets. This method of line retrieval is usually used when fishing wet flies, especially for fast or darting action.

The carefully collected loops allow the angler to start with false casts, shoot line out to get some distance, and do it quickly to get the fly back out.

The palm or hand-twist retrieve is slower and is usually used when fishing dry flies. Again, the line can come down from the stripper guide, over the index finger, to the left hand.

To collect line in the palm of your left hand, start the line running down across your palm from the thumb to the pinkie. With your hand palm side down, bring the thumb over and down so the ball of your thumb and index finger traps the line. Roll your hand counterclockwise so the line forms a loop at the ball of your thumb and lays parallel to the other strand of line.

Fold the three extended fingers over to trap both lines.

Now, you must do two things simultaneously: (1) roll your hand clockwise so the line forms a loose loop around your pinkie, and (2) point your index finger and spread your thumb apart.

Continue to roll your hand clockwise until the line goes across the three fingers and touches the first loop of line.

Close your thumb and forefinger on the line.

Slip your three fingers out of the loop of line you just made, and reversing the roll, open them so they are extended flat again.

You should be back at your beginning mode, but this time with a loop at the top, a loop at the bottom, and three strands of line running across your palm. You will notice, the looser you make the roll-over loops, the easier it will be to slip your fingers out. Practice the retrieve slowly at first, and gradually you will develop speed.

That's it!

Continue to trap, pick-up, and slip-out as long as you need.

When it's time to cast again, drop the line that was running across the index finger, then you can tug and pull and let the line shoot right out from the nicely laid out line in your palm.

Try not to squeeze the loops together because that can cause a snarl.

Either retrieve may be used to take in slackline between the tip of the rod and the fly. A taut line is one of the rudiments of good fishing. A taut line is ready to set a hook or impart action to a fly. It keeps the line under constant, instant control.

18

The Cast Fly

A fly is cast when the angler allows the energy to dissipate from the line to let the line fall and land the fly. Usually, this is done on the frontwards cast. You may remember this is the controlled collapse.

The collapsing cast may occur in three ways:

1. When the angler casts and allows the energy in the line to dissipate.

2. When the angler shoots the line at the same time allowing the line to fly as far as it possibly can before the fly lands on the water; and

3. When the angler adds another impulse in the same direction to make the tippet land "invisibly." (More on this later.)

There is less control with a one-handed shoot-the-line cast if one holds down the fly-line under the middle finger by the handle to make the cast. Then, on the forward cast, as the tug comes on the line, the fisherman releases the line under the finger, which causes the outgoing line to pull out some two or three or four feet of line just before it collapses landing the fly.

Before going any further, the angler may become exceedingly confident if he finds he can fly a length of line at least three times the length of the rod. Keep the line tight under the rod hand. Remember to practice backcasting the line "directly over the head." A point should be made here concerning anglers who strive for distance casts. The fish never knows how much line the angler was able to cast to present the fly. So, the theory is it is far better anytime to make a perfect short cast than a bad long-distance cast.

The next step is to false cast or fly the line two or three times back and forth, then allow the line to land.

To get the line flying again, practicing "plucking a frog" off the surface of the water with the tip of the rod and sending the "frog" straight up over your head. You may remember the angler needs that extra tug to overcome the inertia of the line at rest or the cohesive force of the water to get the line flying again. This downward tug of the line from the stripper guide is the same maneuver used to set the hook.

Should you be told you're bending your wrist too much and told you should be wearing a wrist band, if you pluck the frog correctly, you won't need it. The reason is when you pluck the frog and making the backcast that's supposed to go straight over your head, then the action of your hand on the rod should be as if it moves up in a straight line from your belt to just above your head. Keep the back of your rod hand facing the sky and put some speedy energy into raising your hand as straight upward as you're able. Think of drawing a straight line with the back of your hand from the tips of your shoes, past your nose, and straight-up! That's the action of getting a high backward cast to create a high plane behind you. When you do that, you just can't bring the tip of the rod lower than the two on the clock face.

Here's how to avoid line slippage. Remember your technique of false casting and the tug. If the line was held under the hand holding the handle, the backward pull of the rod—mentioned earlier—would make the topmost guide slip back down the line (toward the reel) for almost a foot because of the flex of the rod before the line was able to get taut and pull directly at the hook. That one-foot slippage can allow the fish to fight free of the hook, which is not set. Said another way, without the downward tug, the line slips through the guides bending the rod not allowing any backward pressure needed to set the hook.

Setting the hook means tugging the line to make the hook go into the fish past the barb of the hook. The barb on the hook prevents the hook from slipping backward out of the fish and losing the catch. Some sportsmen test their skills by using barbless hooks. The fish must be played perfectly, not to lose it. No barb also means less harm to the catch and release fish or from the ear of a hooked fly caster.

A word on "Tight Lines." This is usually an expression of goodwill among fly-fishermen (like "Break a Leg" is in theatre). When one has a fish hooked, the technique is to keep the line taught. A slackline allows the fish to control the fight, to head into the weeds or rocks, under a sunken tree, or deep into a hole. When a fish rises out of the water—and it's just amazing how fish know this—the fish's technique is to slap the hook or the line with its tail to dislodge the darn thing. I always suspected fish broke the surface of the water for more than just to show off. This technique is most successful when the line is tight, as you can understand because it doubles the power of the tail slap and may tear the hook loose. So, to counter these Phi Beta Kappa fish, on a rise the fisherman for that moment allows the line to go slack, usually by lowering the entire rod, not just the tip. Otherwise, Tight Lines to you!

Now get the idea of **coordinating your hands**. Hold the rod in one hand. Hold the line in the other hand, but keep the hand holding the line as close to the stripper guide on the rod as you are able comfortably to do it. The motion here is to have both hands "wave" the rod backward and forward as they remain in the same relative position.

The technique of holding the line hand close to the stripper guide will improve your fly-casting and fly-fishing. Here are the reasons for keeping your hands close together will work for the angler:

1. To acquire the technique to overcome inertia or the cohesive force of water.
2. To help go into a heavy tug for the extra pull needed to shoot line; and
3. To help set the hook when a fish strikes.

In all three of these, the action is to **yank down hard** on the line. This yank or tug is easiest to perform with your line handheld at the highest point it can, which is the stripper guide. The closer to the stripper guide the tug is started, the quicker the action will be felt in the line (and gives you a longer way to exert the tug).

As with any skill, the more correct the practice, the more correct will the skill be acquired. Practice only the ideal technique. Should you become fatigued or lax, stop to regroup, or quit for a while.

At this point, you are ready to cast the line with a **power assist.**

The technique is to tug downwards with the line hand as the rod hand firmly loads the rod by going sharply backward (stretching wide a rubber band held by both hands). The two hands are going pretty much in opposite directions. In effect, the tug of the line pushes the line against the rod, and the rod pushes against the line, which reinforces the action of the line coming in.

If the hands do not work together in this manner, then the tip of the rod will bend as if it is anchored to the water by inertia. It will take in less line and diminish the action needed at the tip of the line. Without both actions, the job of taking up the slack in the line is only half done. Without both actions, the fraction of a second delay in setting the hook may cost the angler a fish. Without both actions, there may not be enough force to overcome water tension to get a long line into the air.

Practice **shooting the line**—still without a hook attached—on the forward cast only. It seems to be the easiest to do. Fly the line with both hands moving together. Then, as you watch the loop behind you, tug down on the line as you bring the rod forward. As the line moves to be in front of you, you will feel the pull of the line. That's the moment to release your hold on the line as if you were trying to push it up through the stripper guide. Allow your hand to follow the line up toward the guide, then, when you see and feel the line is no longer going out, grab the line again, and prepare to tug it again. The first time you coordinate this, you will probably shoot about four feet of line. No matter where the line lands, the important thing is that you get the idea of shooting line. Get the line flying again and do it again. Soon, you'll be able to start with just a short length of line out; then, as you shoot line, you will fly more and more line. You will find this is what you will want to do, especially after you've pulled line in and want to get it back into the air. Or, if you've just tied on a fly and want to get some line out.

It is wise to acquire this skill slowly. The next step is to fly the line, but this time concentrate on shooting the line on the backward cast. At the end of the forward cast—thinking you must send the line straight up over your head—tug the line and pull the rod at the same time, release the line to let it fly out above you, then grab the line again, and continue with the tug and pull for the forward cast.

A reminder: be patient and kind to yourself. Do not expect to shoot yards and yards of line at first. Getting a few feet out correctly will build your confidence and enable you to do better and better. Once you have mastered the skill correctly, it will be like riding a bike: You will not forget how to do it for the rest of your life.

The adage that applies to fly-casting and any skill is:

1. Watch someone do it.
2. Do it yourself; then
3. Teach someone else to do it.

At this point, do not be surprised to know that accuracy—having the fly land at the exact spot you wish it to—is only a few casts away.

As your proficiency with the cast increases, you may wish to practice casting in every direction around you just as you exercised with the ribbon. Know precisely what you wish to do, then do it as if you're teaching someone else how to do it. The fun then is to become a teacher. It's just amazing how it improves your skill because you will be focusing on doing every single thing the very best you are able.

Now you know: Fly-fishing is teaching you.

49. GREEN DRAKE

50. GREY FOX VARIANT

51. HENDRICKSON PARACHUTE

52. SPENT WING

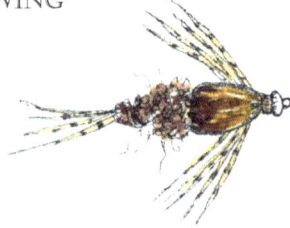

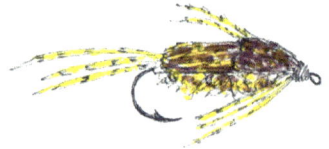

54. DINOS BROWN
NYMPH

53. DINOS PHEASANT
TAIL NYMPH

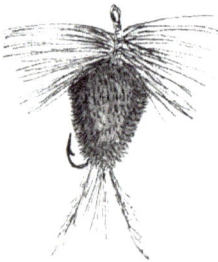

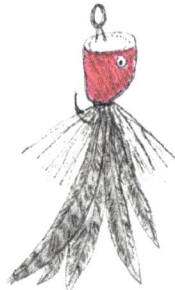

57. MICEY BUG

55. GHOST FROG

56. SHADOW BUG

14

The Roll Cast

The roll cast is basic. It is easy to master. It will be valuable in many different situations, especially if a flying cast is not possible.

To make the roll cast first lay a length of line out before you. Holding the line so it will not slip through the guides, with you facing the three-o'clock position point the rod at the three. It is at this position that **we want the cohesion of the line lying on the water to hold.** This "resistance" is necessary to execute the cast. Then, in one continuous smooth motion with a quick snap, jerk the tip of the rod back over your shoulder to the eleven o'clock position and bring it smartly forward to the two o'clock position and abruptly stop the rod there. In effect, the cohesion holds the line still while the sharp impulse from the rod tip makes a large loop that runs down the entire length of the line. To visualize the action, picture a wheel as tall as your rod at the twelve o'clock position. When you begin the action of your cast, think of catching the top of the wheel and rolling it forward as hard as you can. Your line will form a circle—as you saw the ribbon perform—and "roll" down the line and cast out the tip. The impulse energy you apply on your forward cast must be enough to carry the roll down the entire length of line. If it collapses before the end, then either take in a length of line or use more energy to start the cast.

The angler will use the roll cast when he finds there is no room for a backcast to straighten out the line so it can be picked up and put into the air, to adjust for wind in making a cast, or to mend a cast. Or, to run out more line to prepare for an overhead cast.

After running circles with the ribbon, the roll cast should come easily. After getting the hang of the roll cast, variations should also come as good fun. Change the angle of the roll cast from one side or the other. You may reduce the angle until you are making a sideward cast. A sideward cast is used to get a fly in under overhanging branches, to put a fly under a bridge, or under a dock.

Here are some interesting and fun casts.

We have emphasized the basic casting fact not to counter one impulse with another. A forward impulse will clash with a backward impulse. Don't put the two together. We got that.

Now we will **add an impulse to the line that will go in the same direction.** "Same direction" are the operative words. In addition to the impulse that takes the line out, we will add impulses that will give you three additional fly-casting techniques.

They are turning a corner, the wiggle cast, and humping the fly.

First, these casts are dependent on the basic fact: **"As the rod tip goes, so goes the line."**

Turning a corner.

Make the fly turn a corner when you want to put it behind something like a rock or a stump. First, focus on where you would like to place your fly. Make the usual overhead cast close to your target. Anticipate when the fly is just about where you want it to turn the corner, make the tip of your rod snap—really use a lot of wrist to snap a sharp impulse—in the **sidewise** direction you want it to go, left or right. This is the primary impulse. Then, immediately thereupon, the rod tip itself will add the secondary impulse to wrench the tip back to its original position. This whipping action has been described as a "hiccough." The tip of the rod moves in the shape of the letter "S," but the intensity of the primary or first sidewise snap is much sharper than the second one. The snap does not affect the initial, original impulse that cast the fly because this sidewise snap action is a supplementary impulse that is not contrary to the initial outgoing impulse. It does not affect the original kinetic impulse cast. Another way of explaining the reason is "turns a corner" is that the original loop is going, say, up and down, and the directional impulse is going side to side. Because the primary sidewise impulse is greater than its secondary one, the line will move in that direction with little or no effect of the secondary impulse because the impulse by time it reaches the end of the line it is collapsing or landing.

I can tell you what I told my brother. "If I was smart enough to know what was behind that rock, what in the dickens am I doing up to my butt in the water?"

I should have expected his answer. "Fly-fishing! Don't you love it!"

The Wiggle Cast

I can't remember the last time I used a wiggle cast. I don't think instructors teach it anymore. The action is to impart to the flying line a series of back and forth wiggles to the tip of the rod to make the fly-line land on the water in a series of "S" curves (as the tip goes, so goes the line). The curves eventually straighten out as the line is taken by the current. The wider the wiggles at the tip of the fly rod, the wider the line wiggles of the line on the water. The cast was made to create slack (once called a Slack Cast) in the line to allow the current not to affect the performance of the fly. The cast was made diagonally across a stream or downstream. As I remember, I was told the cast was supposed to be "deadly with wets," whatever that means. I've made such casts just to pat myself on the back that I was able to do it.

Humping the Fly

That's a provocative cast if I ever heard one. This refers to the cast I mentioned earlier that allows the fly to land first, followed by the tippet slowly folding itself into the water. To hump the fly, the tip of the rod is wrist-snapped once up and down as the line is flying for a landing. Here, again, we are adding a complementary kinetic impulse to the line. Instead of sending a loop down the line, it sends down an in-line "bump" made by the up and down motion. This lengthwise arc runs down the line. The leading point of the arc first reaches the leader, then the tippet, and then the fly where the impulse ends and causes the fly to land. The other end of the arc is controlled by the ending impulse energy of the line, which collapses a split second after the fly touches the water and a hairsbreadth before the impulse ends in the tippet, which energy causes the tippet to hump. Said another way, the weight and ending impulse causes the fly to land on the water before the rearward arc does. Because the dying impulse is still working the knot of the tippet, it moves a bit toward the fly before it, too, lands. In effect, it squeezes the rearward ending arc in the tippet toward the fly and forms the hump.

I understand humping the fly is unnecessary if the cast and the impulse is a smooth portamento—a musical term that means flowing delicately—from rod to line to leader to fly. I've done it both ways and prefer to see fly-fishing done with a light, delicate touch where the end of the line lands, and the fly gently floats down to the water, leaving a hump in the tippet.

The fact is, anything you could do with the rod and the ribbon, you can do with the fly line. Remember making a series of circles? Just try it while you're flying line. Be brave! Make a cast then as the line is going out—zip! The tip of your rod in a circle or two. What happens? Why the line follows, of course! You'll be surprised. Your friends will start calling you a trick fly-caster.

The fact is, in all the time you are fishing, you may never, ever need to cast around a corner, do a wriggle cast, or hump a fly, but knowing how to do it, that's the key. It makes you feel you have an arsenal of skills just like a professional and that you're having a good time, which is what fly-fishing is all about. Also, it counters the wag that said, "Fish should only be caught only by those who know how to fish."

Be sure, if you can cast a line, tie on a fly, or string a rod, you know how to fish.

58. FLIPPER BUG

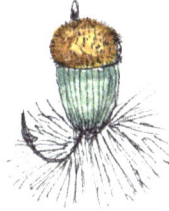

59. BABY FROG

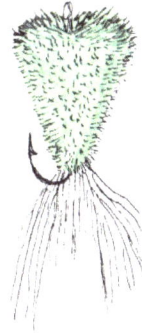

60. CRITTER BUG

61. TREE DROP

62. HURT FROG

63. FROGGY POPPER

64. HURT BUG

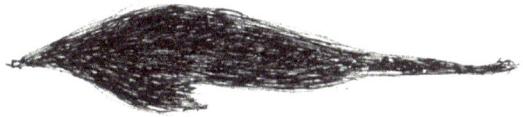

65. LEECH

66. DINOS GHOST STREAMER

15

Leaders, Tippets, and Knots

Before you tie on a fly, you should have some understanding of leaders, tippets, and **knots.**

The correct knot tied adequately is crucial in fly casting. Flies, fish, and time are lost to poor knots. It is worth every second to tie a knot properly. Any knot is a weak point. A properly tied knot can retain 98% of the line's strength. Losing a fish or a fly because a knot becomes untied is pitiful.

One of your best investments will be to buy a book or pamphlet that deals only with knots. Knots are critical. You should learn to tie them from a master. Practice them while you're watching TV or commuting to work until tying a proper knot is second nature.

For safety's sake, never fly-fish without wearing glasses or some form of eye protection. A cast fly flicking a leaf, caught by a breeze, or a not-so-good cast may send it whipping back at you, wrapping itself around your head, and causing an injury. Also, a brimmed hat is excellent protection against a fly hooking an ear.

16

Entomology

Fly-casting is all about delivering an artificial fly or a lure to a fish.

Artificial flies have their foundation in entomology.

Entomology is the foundation of fly fishing.

Entomology is the branch of zoology that deals with insects.

Insects, because that's what sporting fishes eat, especially aquatic insects, those that need water for part of their life's cycle.

If they ate hamburgers, we'd have hamburger fishing, and we'd tie artificial hamburger flies. Entomology is essential because it tells us exactly what type and stage of insects are available to the fishes at what time of year or day. Without entomology, it would be like trying to sell spinach sandwiches to kids.

If we know what the fishes are eating, we know what to serve them. And there's the catch.

The three primary food sources for fish in the water are mayfly, caddisfly, stonefly.

Wherever you are going to fish, it's got to be a little different than any other place. Talk to fly fishermen about the area, about the flies that have worked for them at what time of day. Join a fishing club. You may be at the mercy of the sporting goods salesman, but he or she wants you to come back and will make sincere suggestions. Then, because you don't want to spend your retirement money to cover all possible fly patterns—compromise! Ask for the four most popular dry flies used in the area and get them in two sizes. If you can afford it, buy two of each. As you acquire experience, you are bound to lose flies. If you lose a fly to a bad snap or a tree, you'll be glad you have a spare. But! If you lose a fly to a ferocious fish, you'll guard its twin with acquired wisdom and skill. Also, get six of the most popular wet flies, and, if recommended for the local waters, add a bucktail, streamer, or popper. Unless you get into fly tying this will be your supply of flies—replacing any as you lose—for this, your first season

With the flies, get all the information you are able on the leader that works best in that area. Don't buy too many. You may wish to go to another length or style that suits you better.

All of this to suggest that just before you tie that first fly on your line that you study the water world about you. Knowing that there is a definite behavior about the fishes' food supply, look at what's on or in the water, or under rocks; what activity is taking place. It is incumbent on you to do some studying on and off the stream if you wish to have a further and fuller understanding of the sport.

An angler just can't load up his refrigerator with all kinds of shapes and sizes and stages of aquatic insects to use at fishing time. Besides, they would be useless because aquatic insects do not print programs of exactly what time they're going to do what thing. Just as Bostonians prefer baked beans to collard greens, fishes in the next stream over, or another part of the country prefer a different specie or size of insect. So, the easiest and smartest thing to do is to lay in a supply of artificial insects in all stages, sizes, colors called artificial flies which are supposed to represent the real thing—dry when it's out of the water, wet when it's in the water. Artificial because they're fake, not the real thing. And fly because they are made to move through the air as well as the fact that a fly is also an insect.

You might say the fly tier is the chef of fly fishing. As the angler, it's your task through education, experience, guesswork, luck to select the particular fly, of a particular size, of a particular color for a particular body of water, at a particular time of day, to fish in a particular spot and make a catch. I think you're beginning to understand. If you are not meticulous about anything else unless you want to constantly rely on "by guess and by gosh," you will be very careful when it comes to selecting a fly to tie onto your line so that you may become as smart as the fish. Believe it or not, there isn't that much quality fishing time, no matter when you get to the water. This is true only for fly fishing. So, be present, be alert, think your actions through, and give the fly you are about to tie on your line considered thought. As in any sport, the keyword is "focus." Although it's pleasant to think of your Saturday night date, better you leave that action for Saturday night and focus on what you're doing standing in a stream with a fly rod in hand.

A valid point to make about all of this is that we do not think you must get a degree in entomology to be a good fly fisherman. This is the basic information one needs to be intelligent about concerning this marvelous sport. I've spoken with fly fishermen who did not understand what artificial flies were all about. To them, flies were flies. They were used instead of worms. They had no idea they represented the food that the fishes ate. As they say, don't learn just enough about what fishes eat to get you in trouble. No, learn just enough to make it more fun!

The types of flies are mayflies; attractors; caddisflies; dragons/damsels/crane flies; leeches/worms; midges; salmon flies/stoneflies; scuds/shrimp/sowbugs; terrestrials.

Fishing flies generally fall into one of six classifications. There are hundreds of different patterns and variations in their design and construction. One catalog listed these varieties of flies: Mayfly Lifecycle, Hare's Ear, Prince, Terrestrial, Emerger, Wooly Buggers, Hooper Copper Dropper, Adams Family, Rising Trout, Bead Head and Tungsten Nymph, and Klinkhammer. Whew! Fly tiers are quick to design a new fly of one sort or another and name it after a grandchild. A fly-tier invented a fly he called a "bi-visible" because it could be seen by both the fish and the fisherman. Over the years, it has endured because it is a proven fish catcher. Here's a general list:

- **Dry flies**. Dry flies are designed to float on the surface of the water. The lure imitates or represents insects that, for one reason or another, land on, leave, or come up to the surface of the water.

- **Wet flies**. Fish do most of their feeding underwater. Wet flies are made to represent insects/foods that are underwater. It represents an insect that spends part of its life submerged, an insect that has died, one that is emergent or hatching on the bottom and rising to the surface or may be indigenous prey such as leeches.

- **Streamers and bucktails**. Streamers are designed with feathers. Bucktails use deer hair. They are wet flies designed to imitate a minnow or baitfish, the action of which is initiated by the angler and not just the water.

- **Nymphs**. Nymphs are created to imitate aquatic insects that are to emerge as adults that rise through the water to the surface. Trout love them. Fishing nymphs take a great deal of skill, requiring a good bit of study to know exactly how they are to be fished—wet, dry, or on the bottom of deep holes.

- **Terrestrials.** These are manna from heaven for the fish. They're supposed to represent land-based insects that just have fallen or are blown onto the water. These may include grasshoppers, ants, crickets, beetles, cicadas. I watched a red squirrel fall out of a tree, land in the water, and WHOMP became lunch for a bass!

- **Poppers**. These are surface lures that represent water or terrestrial food that are irresistible because their action usually is that of a wounded tidbit.

- **MATCH THE HATCH.** "Match the hatch" is the admonition given to fly fishermen that they should use artificial flies that resemble the plentiful insects that the fish just happen to be feeding on at that time. These insects generally have reached the stage where they (hatch) leave their "casings" on the bottom of the brook, river, or pond and rise through the water to the surface where they are taken by fish. Or, they could be insects that land on the surface, dive to the bottom to lay eggs, then resurface. No matter what their source, the trick is to be savvy enough to be able to identify the hatch and pray you have a fly in your box that somewhat matches the size and coloration of the hatch. A note: Hatches change hour by day. What was on today will be different tomorrow.

An added dimension to fly-fishing is **to tie your flies.**

Fly tying is an art and a science. It requires skill and creativity. The skill may be acquired in a relatively short time. To become a master fly-tier may take years upon years, for instance, to match curls, colors, and cuts. Creativity allows the imagination to add to the creation or duplication of a fly that has already been made.

A fly is tied on a hook. Hooks come in all sizes, styles, and shapes.

In tying a fly, the tier will first select the size hook he wants to use depending on what kind of a fly he wants to create. Different flies are tied in different manners, using different kinds of materials, which range from feathers to animal hair, artificial material, to wire and beads.

It is a unique bit of excitement when you catch a fish on a fly you've tied.

17

The Flies in This Treatise

If a poll were taken of ten fly-fishermen for their ten favorite flies, my guess is we would have a list of 100 different flies.

A hint: Flies are tied by novice and expert alike. Qualities vary. Buy your flies by reputation, not price. The time to check out a dry fly is not at the water's edge, but at home when you can drop it into a glass of water. You will know everything you have to know if a dry fly that's supposed to float sinks to the bottom.

Talk to an experienced fly-fisherman about how to take care of flies. They should be cleaned and dried before being stored in a box. Even a hungry trout will resist a moldy fly or maybe not.

A fly-fisherman pointed out to me five fly-fishing fly boxes in the pockets of his vest. His estimate was they held about 600 flies. My guess was he also had a special divining rod for choosing which one he was going to use at any given moment. My mind could not extrapolate that to the total number of flies in fishermen's boxes all over the country.

The reason illustrations of classic flies are in this treatise is so that anyone who has never seen a fishing fly will have an idea of what we're talking about. They are a minute, arbitrary sampling of the hundreds upon thousands that have been created. And I will always get remarks such as, "But you didn't include the Mickey Finn fly!" These flies are included for the artistic and informational foundation they provide and as an example of what some fly tiers deemed representational of their entomological counterparts in times past.

I consider the entomological illustrations a vital part of this treatise. They provide a trove of information not usually found in other similar works. They offer a foundation for understanding the basis of what this valuable, pleasurable sport is all about.

Modern flies may resemble their entomological inspirations more closely. They have names such as Copper Johns, Hare's Ear nymphs, sulfurs, stimulators. Some have combinations of colors that heat the blood of these cold-water fish that make them strike. We have not included illustrations of modern, contemporary flies. Vera was available to put brush to paper. We barely touch upon them because information, history, usage, and photographs are just so available. Should you search the Internet for fly-fishing flies, you will likely come up with at least ten search engines and at least twenty websites at the first go. My guess is, on my first try, I ran through at least 1,000 modern flies of all sorts and descriptions, and new ones come out every season. If that isn't enough, then use any of the search engines to get catalogs from the myriad of fishing supplies companies. You will get hours upon hours of reading material. The choices will boggle the mind.

Old, new—which will catch more fish?

Only the fly fisherman casting his line over the water to the quarry knows.

18

Compromise and Adjustment

Compromise and adjustment are keywords to remember when you are dealing with fly-fishing as well as life.

In fly-fishing, it refers to making a concession. It refers to accepting something less than ideal, a simple matter of practicality, the formula for which is time matched against the result. The admonition is *Tempus Fugit*, which I translate to, "Time is my enemy."

In fly-fishing, there is always a compromise and adjustment to be made either in equipment or conditions or your mind-set.

The ideal fly rod has never been made and never will be. So, we compromise and adjust to what is available. The same with fly lines, leaders, tippets, and flies. Anglers have not been asleep on this matter. Fly rods have been made that cost thousands of dollars. Then, we find there is no fly line to match that ideal. So, we compromise and adjust. All this to say, there is an infinite variety of fly-fishing equipment. The ideal is what suits you and whether you can afford it. As you become more and more proficient, you will find yourself looking for better, more ideal equipment. That is the recommended way to approach the sport. A wisp of a one-piece rod of beauty in the hands of a neophyte can end up snapped into pieces. A fishing friend or the salesperson in the local sporting goods store is the perfect place to start. Sure, cheaper through mail order or the Internet, perhaps, but you need the personal feedback at this stage. In all price ranges, there is an infinite variety of rods, lines, reels, leaders, tippets, flies, and lures, which the salesperson might not know completely. Should you buy just one outfit, remember it will have to do for a variety of situations, accepting adjustment and compromise. It must serve you for wet and dry flies and lures; fishing from a bank or a canoe or stream or river; on calm or windy days; for brook trout or bass. And all that before you get into conditions involving wind, weather, and water. The salesman will know that, and because he or she knows the area, he will be the best source of advice. He should be knowledgeable about the best flies to use in the area. Buy as wide a variety of all the types as your budget will allow. Besides, he may allow you to try out several outfits so you can experiment with the search for the best compromise for you. If the salesperson is real smart, the strong suggestion will be made to buy this *Treatise*. No matter what the rod, or line, or leader, master it first, then move on to the next.

Adjusting to all these compromises is what will make you, the fisherperson, what you want to be. Just as it is in life, enjoying the process is fun.

Fly-fishing . . . Ah! What a concept!

Acknowledgments

The adage, "There are acres of diamonds in your backyard," has never been more accurate. I found in my family the esponsibility for this volume's foundation and development. I am indebted to my older brother, Dino, a professional hobbyist, who retired as an engineer working interstellar communications. As a five-year-old, he taught me how to put a worm, then a crayfish, then a minnow on a hook. Finally, he taught me the magic of an artificial fly. With meticulous patience, he explained then showed me the mechanics of fly-casting. In awe, I watched him tie a fly on a Number 22 (tiny!) hook, which he held in his fingers—not a vice! —as his nimble hands went to work. My bride, Vera, spent countless hours and tons of energy in meticulously rendering and painting fish, flies, terrestrials. My younger daughter, Mona, made editorial suggestions and corrections that lifted this volume higher than my expectations. New-found fly-fishing guru Gary Spielmann allowed me to plagiarize his concepts. Is there a greater love of fly-fishing? Dear friend Gene Hunter who had my six in a myriad of life's doings, returns with my gratitude. I excuse myself for anything erroneous, or anything I misremembered, or anything I didn't get right in this book, including the names of flies, lures, poppers, nymphs, and such, or others inasmuch as I had no other sources except as I found them to be. Also, because I still need help spelling physics. Life is to be enjoyed, and fly-fishing is one of the ingredients.

—Paul Argentini

PLATE D. BROOK TROUT

Index

About the Author

Paul and Vera Argentini

PAUL ARGENTINI was a Random House best-selling author and prize-winning playwright. He and his bride, Vera, lived in Florida. They have two grown daughters, Lisa and Mona.

www.ingramcontent.com/pod-product-compliance
Lightning Source LLC
Chambersburg PA
CBHW051214090426
42742CB00022B/3453